GOOD COMPANY:
Poets from Grinnell College

"Writers need company. We all need it. It's not the command of knowledge that matters finally, but the company. It's the predecessors. As a writer, I don't know where I'd be without them."

—Amy Clampitt '41
(from a talk given in Herrick Chapel, Grinnell College, February 1986)

Predecessors, Et Cetera,
Essays by Amy Clampitt,
Ann Arbor,
University of Michigan Press, 1991

GRINNELL COLLEGE
GRINNELL, IOWA

On the cover: *Grand Case*, Richard Cervene '51,
1971, oil on canvas, 65" x 65", Grinnell College
Faulconer Gallery permanent collection.

DEDICATION

The title for this book was suggested to me by words spoken at a writers' symposium in Herrick Chapel by Amy Clampitt '41. This collection of poems by alumni of Grinnell College is dedicated to her memory.

Acknowledgments

My pleasure in working on this book has included the enjoyment and benefit of some very good company. I asked a lot from many people in putting it together, and I should like to thank them here.

Jim Powers, director of publications at Grinnell College, expertly designed an attractive volume and was sensitive and long-suffering in dealing with the editor's whims, second thoughts, and shortcomings. Jim's colleagues in the Office of Public Relations, Mickey Munley, the director, and Jackie Hartling Stolze, were both patient and encouraging. The arduous and painstaking work of keying in the text was admirably accomplished by Martha Pinder '84. The vital task of proofreading was carefully executed by Cheryl Neubert, by Barbara '64 and Russell Tabbert, and by Nancy Kissane '52. Anita Schrodt assumed the complex assignment of securing permissions to publish copyrighted material. Leslie Czechowski and Catherine Rod, college archivists, were invaluable in researching the work and lives of the earlier poets, and the same goes for my student helper Pranita Sharma '02. President Russell K. Osgood was extraordinarily supportive of this project, and his wife Paula Osgood's knowledge of and interest in Grinnell's poets made her encouragement especially welcome.

My particular thanks go to every one of the living contributors to this volume. It was a joy to renew many friendships and make new ones among these gracious and gifted people. Obviously it is their work, and that of their predecessors, that made this book possible.

Table of Contents

Introduction

This is a book for Grinnellians. It is a selection from
the work over the past 100 years and more by poets, all
of whom attended Grinnell College. It is not a collec-
tion of student poetry; it is by no means a book of
poems about Grinnell (though the college is recogniz-
ably present in two or three of them). All of the poets
represented are not equally well-known to readers of
poetry; of course their work is diverse and will not
appeal equally to everyone. No doubt this anthology
reflects different levels of accomplishment, just as it
reveals a wide variety of styles and subject matter. Every
writer included is a published poet; most of the poems
here have previously appeared in print, but I have
thought it would enhance the value and interest of this
collection to include some work published here for the
first time. Somewhat reluctantly—but consistent with
my aim—I ruled out work by members of Grinnell's
faculty, except in the case of those poets who taught at
the college as well as attended it as students.

I suppose—in fact I hope—that whatever interest
Grinnellians may take in such a volume will be of many
different kinds. Some will search it for poems by people
they knew as fellow students. Some will be curious to
consider how these poems by generations of writers, all
from their alma mater, match—or do not match—with
the ideas about what poetry is and does they themselves
remember having largely acquired or developed during
their years in college. Some will particularly note the

2   sweep of time this collection covers and be freshly reminded that the college we knew as relatively stable and innocent helped produce such a range of historical experience and human response. Some may look for signs of an elusive and ineffable but essential "Grinnellishness." Others may simply like to reflect on so much variety, so many different ways of looking at the world and expressing oneself, having had at least one thing—and probably a crucially formative thing—in common.

As I put together this anthology, obvious and annoying questions kept bearing in upon me: What's the point of making the college they attended the basis on which to assemble work by a group of different poets? Would a comparable collection of poetry by graduates of Williams or Reed or Carleton look much different from what we have here? Is this collection supposed to illustrate anything true and worth knowing about the particular college all these very different poets attended? Are there traditions or teachers or experiences peculiar to Grinnell that contributed to making some of its students into poets?

In light of such questions, I have sometimes felt that my project could be no more reasonably justified than could a collection of Poems by Stamp Collectors, or Poems by People Who Have Never Visited Italy. Yet I remain convinced it is a thing worth doing: a bringing together of poems by writers I wanted to see in each other's company. As I developed my list of poets to be represented, all of those I could reach by a letter describing the sort of anthology I had in mind told me they liked the scheme and were happy to cooperate in it. Perhaps the only thing that unanimous response told me for certain was that poets hardly ever mind seeing their work in print. In any event it spurred me on. As for the annoying questions, I have no convincing answers; but pondering them as I collected the poems in this volume, I have at least come to a few thoughts.

One thought has to do with the fact that Grinnell, like other good colleges, has always put a high value on the activity of writing. Writing is a widely useful skill; it is also one of the most accessible of the fine arts. As such, it produces in those who attempt to practice it, like any art, frequent frustration and anguish but also excitement and deep satisfaction. The more a college recognizes writing as an essential skill, the more it should also emphasize it as a pleasure-giving art. Colleges like Grinnell have always done so; they have encouraged such activities as writing clubs, sponsored writing contests, included nonutilitarian writing as part of the curriculum, supported college literary magazines, and brought to their campuses, for brief appearances or longer visits, accomplished writers of all kinds to interact with, instruct, and inspire their students.

As a result of these and other efforts, a college like Grinnell tends to produce two crucially significant, strongly contrasting, but ultimately complementary effects upon many of its students. One such effect is that these students come to hold writing and those who are good at it in very high regard. The other—I'm tempted to call it the *opposite*—effect is to make such an art seem, certainly not ordinary, but nonetheless

4   *natural.* Writing that aspires to the exacting standards of
an art is thereby both valorized and familiarized by a
college environment—students are encouraged to think
of excellent writing as not only wonderful but even
possible.

A story has it that an English teacher, who
happened to be a talented poet, would occasionally, to
make some legitimate point or other, read to his class
one of his own poems. A student once confounded and
delighted him after one such reading by asking, "Sir,
was that a *real* poem, or did you make it up?"

When Mike Liberman would tell that story in his
incomparable way, it was always good for a laugh. Yet
come to think of it, isn't it possible to see in that joke,
not "more truth than poetry," perhaps, but a truth
more revealing than an imaginary student's ridiculous
naiveté? Funny as it is, Mike's joke manages to lay
hands on and harness together those two contrasting
attitudes toward poetry in the academy that I have
referred to and that justify what Marianne Moore calls
"all this fiddle" about it in departments of literature and
in colleges like Grinnell.

Whether he knows it or not, that mythical
student's question reveals an assumption and implies a
contrasting discovery about poetry, and in so doing
pays it two unintended and equally valuable tributes:
first, that it is very "far out," as we used to say, and
second, that it is also very close to home. Magical and
august indeed, yet natural and everyday; an odd and
surprising display of language that nevertheless touches
our sense of what was always already there.

"*Is that a* real *poem, or did you make it up?*" he asks.
On the one hand, such a question certainly assumes
that *real* poems are nothing like the stuff of everyday
experience. We have a word for that all-too-familiar
level of experience, and the word is *prosaic*, the absolute
opposite—so it would seem—of the "poetic." The
poetic—everybody since Plato has known—inhabits
the realm of the essential, is after all more "true" even
than history. How is it possible to imagine such truth to
be merely "made up"? Surely anything so rare and fine
can not have been created by anyone as ordinary, as
many worlds away from the "ideally real," as this
agreeable enough but completely prosaic individual
who stands in front of us three hours each week here in
this classroom in ARH? Here we read and discuss
poems that have been and will be discussed by genera-
tions of students, poems linked to names that will be
remembered forever. "What you have read to us just
now," that make-believe student must have been
thinking, "was it *theirs*—or is it merely yours?" (*Was it a
vision or a waking dream?*)

That imaginary student is every student in a
college like Grinnell who confronts the strange and
inspiring dichotomy implicit in having poetry—which
stands here for all the arts—brought out of the clouds,
as it were, and displayed among us, without losing its
glamour. "The light that never was, on sea or land"
made to shine in and upon perfectly familiar people
and places and things, and in that way made to seem
not less extraordinary but more achievable.

This happens—at least there is a chance of its

6   happening—any day in the classroom. But colleges also
make it happen more dramatically. There is the literary
magazine, for instance, where aspiring writers actually
experience the dangerous and delicious thrill of seeing
their own words in print. Another instance—let me call
it in the words of Browning's poem, the "Ah,-did-you-
once-see-Shelley-plain?" instance—is the appearance of
well-known writers on campus. Such memorable
appearances give students rich moments, including
some that will seem trivial to many—seeing Randall
Jarrell playing tennis with one's instructor, or catching a
glimpse of Professor Charlie Foster strolling out into
the countryside one warm spring day in the company
of Robert Penn Warren and what looked like a bottle of
Tennessee bourbon.

An especially important instance of a poet on
campus during my undergraduate years at Grinnell was
the appearance of Robert Frost as a guest at the Writers'
Conference my freshman year. He read to us many of
those poems everybody knows while we literally sat at
his feet. Then he told us, among other things, an
amusing and pointed story about Ezra Pound helpfully
offering to work over some of Frost's own newly written
poems with a view to ridding them of all the excess
words Pound was sure he could find. ("Yes!" I remem-
ber Mr. Frost laughing, "And he'd have thrown out my
meaning too!")

I'm claiming no epiphanic virtue in such mo-
ments—alas, they certainly failed to make me into a
poet!—but they typify something all students need and
that colleges like Grinnell are so well-suited to supply: a

sense that an artist—in this case a poet—is neither
more nor less than what Wordsworth claimed: a man—
or woman, I think I can hear his sister Dorothy
correcting him tartly—speaking to men. Colleges like
Grinnell provide the ideal occasions where the young
can feel poetry, as it were, very close at hand, not only
making its big noises but showing its reassuring
humanity.

One of the ways a college should think of itself is as a
place that helps its students go on to do a range of
interesting and worthy things. Many of these achieve-
ments get the attention, the recognition, they deserve;
some never will. It has long been my opinion that
Grinnell has "produced" or "turned out" (though such
phrases misrepresent the relation of alma mater to her
children) an impressive number of accomplished
writers. More than might be supposed, given the fact
that Grinnell is not perceived—nor does it so consider
itself—as "a creative writing place." It is in other areas
of endeavor—public service, for instance, science,
academic administration, and the law—where Grinnell
graduates seem to most of us to have made a dispropor-
tionately impressive mark. In the guise of a collection of
poetry written over more than a century, this volume is
a reminder that, for a long time, people have come
through Grinnell College who are serious about and
accomplished in the art of writing. That includes of
course many other kinds of writing besides poetry; but
a collection of these other kinds would be a clumsy
affair if not altogether a hopeless project.

8   So this collection of poems, it's my hope, is a kind
of synecdoche (now there's an English professor's word
for you!) for all the writing Grinnellians have produced
in a wide variety of forms. Accomplished writers of
prose—fiction, history, biography, cultural studies, and
so on—may feel this is too distant or oblique an
acknowledgment of their work. If so, I can only say that
as I enjoyed putting together this anthology of poems I
often thought of other Grinnellians whose other kinds
of writing I have admired over many years—Joe Wall
'41, Gary Giddins '70, Robert Cantwell '66, Rebecca
Hill '66, Sam Tanenhaus '77, Benjamin Barber '60, R.
J. ("Tex") Kaufman '47, Phillip Hallie '44, Caroline
Scheaffer Arnold '66, Margaret Currier Boylen, Andrew
Billingsly '51, Kathleen Snow '65, Margaret McMullan
'82, Terry Bisson '64, Peter (Cohon) Coyote '64, Lucia
Lynner Nevai '67. I can't name them all.

And while offering this collection as a part that
implies a still more impressive whole, may I also express
the hope that the poets and poetry in this book can be a
reminder of other extremely worthwhile verse-writing
by Grinnellians I have not included. There are those
who write poetry and, for whatever reasons, do not
publish it. I know for sure there is a lot of such writing.
It is a very good thing to do, and I suspect one reason
you do it (whether or not you realize this) may be that
you attended Grinnell College.

Then there are the Grinnell writers who do meet
my self-imposed criterion of being "published" poets,
but whom I have inadvertently overlooked. Accept my
apology; I should have searched more thoroughly.

Maybe next time. Maybe a new and expanded edition
of this volume in time for Grinnell's bicentennial in the
year 2046. Why not?

— James Kissane '52
Athens, Ga.
January 2000

10

George Meason Whicher 1882 11

Born in 1860 in Muscatine, Iowa, George Meason
Whicher was one of the surviving members of Grinnell
College's "cyclone class" of 1882. Preparatory to what
was to be a career very much in the "old school" model
as a teacher-scholar of classical languages and an able
poet, Whicher received postgraduate education at The
Johns Hopkins University and Columbia University
and an honorary Litt.D. degree from Iowa College (as
Grinnell was officially known in those days) in 1905.

After having taught classics at Hastings College in
Nebraska, Lawrenceville School in New Jersey (as
"classical master"), and the Packer Collegiate Institute
in Brooklyn, he was appointed professor and head of
the Department of Greek and Latin at Hunter College
in New York City. He remained at Hunter for 25 years,
and during that time served three years as president of
the New York Archaeological Society and in 1921 was
in charge of the Classical School of the American
Academy in Rome. Professor Whicher's retirement
years, from 1924 until his death in 1937, were spent
with his wife (Lillian Frisbie, a Grinnell classmate) in
Amherst, Mass., next door to his son, the noted
authority in American literature George F. Whicher,
and his family.

In addition to a good deal of scholarly writing and
lecturing, George M. Whicher published three books of
poetry between 1912 and 1935. His work, which
appears to be virtually untouched and untroubled by

12   anything like the Modern Spirit, reveals a marked gift
for the writing of well-formed sonnets and ingratiating
light verse.

LANG SYNE

Yo-ho, my wailing Damon! have done with thy
    complaining,
      Cease thy feigning broken-heartedness, and pipe a
      cheerier tune;
Let us sing old songs together, twenty winter snows
    disdaining;
      Sunny weather floods the woods again and we are
      young–in June.

O-ho! for the glorious river, flowing softly, flowing ever,
      With the quiver of southeast breezes all the long,
      long afternoon;
With the glinting, rippling reaches where the sand-bar,
      faintly showing,
      Foretold the beaches rising when the waters fall in
      June.

O-ho! for the far off ridges with the oak groves thinly
    sloping
      To the bridges where the rivulets a shrunken ditty
      croon;
For the minnow swiftly dashing and the crayfish
    fiercely groping;
      For the splashing idle hours away in never ending
      June.

14   Sing hey! for the dusty highway! Sing the slow return-
                    ing journey!
                Shady byway, windy slope, and rocky glen with
                    moss bestrewn;
            For the rare imagined treasure hid in thickets dark and
                    ferny;
                O what measure costing, wasting, from our wealth
                    of golden June!

            Ho-ho! for the island prairie with the purple bluffs
                    infolded;
                For wild cherry blossoms falling in the currentless
                    lagoon!
            Sing the mossy turtle basking on a log so dank and
                    molded:–
                Who is asking more than sunshine and to be alive
                    in June?

TO BE FORGOTTEN   **15**

Why should to be forgotten grieve me so
    When these dull eyes have seen their last of light?
    Am I a silly child that dreads the night
When it must leave its broken toys and go?
Do then so many love me now? or know
    How precious their remembrance in my sight?
    This I endure; why then, in reason's spite,
Why should to be forgotten grieve me so?

Yet I do grieve. This aching pinch of dust,
That I call me,–these foolish, foiled desires–
Mourns that the Sum of Things betrays my trust;
That Time, which lit the flame, will quench the fires,
So soon recalling what unasked he gave,
And I lie darkling, nameless, in the grave.

I HAVE FORGOTTEN MUCH

I have forgotten much that life has shown
    Of wonder and of glory and of might;
    The loveliness that passes from my sight
Is one with beauty I have never known.
In vain I strive to make my very own
    Music and colors that have caused delight.
    Dull brain! slow heart! In my own will's despite
I have forgotten much that life has shown.

Yet through the shrouding of oblivious years,
    That veil the things that were with things that are,
Poignant as daybreak after midnight tears
    Two things I keep clear-imaged as a star:
The sweet face of my mother when she smiled;
The gaze–blue-eyed, heart-breaking–of a dying child.

AMITY STREET 17

Amherst Town is a fair old town,
Where currents of life flow up and down,–
Up and down through quiet ways
Year after year of cheerful days.
A dim blue coronal of hills
All her wide horizon fills;
But the central pulse of her being beats
At the corner of Pleasant and Amity Streets.

Pleasant Street is known to fame;
Everybody has heard its name.
Many a fine sight there is seen:
The City Hall and the shady Green,
Lord Jeffrey's Inn, and Fraternity Halls,
Offices, stores, and luncheon stalls.
From north to south its smooth ways bend,
With a College astride at either end;
And work and play and business meet
On the pleasant walks of Pleasant Street.

Amity Street goes silently down
The old-time path to Hampton Town,
Curving and wide, airy and still,
On the sunny slope of the westward hill.
Tall elms cast their flickering shade;
Orioles swing there unafraid.
Gold and scarlet the maples burn
Each year when the frosts return;
But every season it's easy to greet
Good friends and true on Amity Street.

18

Few are the roads that might compete
With the tranquil ease of Amity Street.
There you will find, if you will but look,
Many a hidden garden nook
Gay with blossoms, healing with peace,
Where cares are stilled and questions cease;
Many a gleaming ingle fire
Lights to the Land of Heart's Desire.
Oh, a harbor safe, a glad retreat,
Is an Amherst home on Amity Street!

INVITATION

Come hither, Friends; wee have layered uppe
A bite to eat, a drop to suppe;
Here's dry olde oke-wood for a fire,
A quishen'd chair before the hearth;
Then staye not; 'tis our hearts' desire
To have you here at *Stonie Garth!*

20   THE SECRET

Friend of my friend to whom this goes,
Hark to a secret the Poet knows:

Out in the wide world songs he sends.
Will they live or die? Ask his friend's friends' friends.

Selden L. Whitcomb 1887   **21**

Selden Lincoln Whitcomb was born in Grinnell, Iowa, in 1866. He graduated from Grinnell College in 1887 and later studied at Columbia, Cornell, Harvard, Chicago, Colorado, and Washington. After teaching at an academy in Kansas and at Iowa State Teachers College, Whitcomb returned to Grinnell in 1895 to become professor of English literature. During the 10 years he taught at his alma mater, interest and activity in the writing of poetry grew markedly, and *The Unit*, a literary magazine that continued into the mid-1920s, provided a stimulating outlet for creative writing of various kinds by students and faculty, including Whitcomb himself. In 1905 he became professor of English and comparative literature at the University of Kansas where he continued to teach and write poetry until his death in 1930.

Whitcomb was the author of several books of verse and scholarly works on English drama and modern prose fiction. The annual Selden Whitcomb Poetry Contest was established in his honor and continues to award generous cash prizes for the best poems by Grinnell students judged by outstanding poets from around the country.

The bulk of Whitcomb's poetry demonstrates admirable facility in handling a variety of verse forms, rather intricate rhythms, and traditional rhyme schemes. It isn't surprising that he was able to instill in many students the idea of verse writing as a demanding

22   craft. Despite the workmanlike qualities of his own
poetry, it shows a limited originality. Whitcomb seems
too often drawn to the shopworn diction and over-
blown emotionalism typical of late romanticism. His
more ambitious poems, charged with earnest piety, do
not wear as well as some of his less weighty, more lyrical
efforts (some of which move tentatively in the direction
of *fin de siecle* style). Such poetry gives one an illumi-
nating glimpse of the tastes in verse that must have
been broadly reflected in colleges like Grinnell at the
end of the 19th and the beginning of the 20th century.

The last poem included here, "The Path Makers,"
published in *Poetry* in 1924, is of interest as a belated
attempt at *vers libre* in deliberately unadorned language.
But it is the work of someone who has discarded an old
and familiar set of tools in favor of newer ones, which,
though intelligently used, produce in his hands an
uncharacteristically clumsy result.

AFTER THE THEATER   **23**

With heart exultant in the sweet
    True womanhood of Imogen,
I strolled at midnight on the street,
    To mingle with my fellow-men.

And soon in temple-shadow passed
    The lingering woman's bold salute,
And felt my vision fading fast
    Before the presence of the brute.

Ah, would to God it were the truth
    I dreamed before the storied stage!
And only feverish eyes of youth
    That read amiss the living page!

24   "QUESTI, CHE MAI DA ME NON FIA DIVISO"

Though never in sad human story,
    Never dreamed in the visions of song,
Purer passion than ours–may its glory
    Veil the face of the Scorner, the Strong?

In our agonized joy we fear it,
    Crying out in the darkness for trust
That the loving of spirit by spirit
    Dissolve not with dust into dust.

When the arms that have yearned and enfolded,
    Desiring to clasp thee for aye
Lie motionless, hidden and molded,
    Beneath the foul clinging of clay;

When the sweetness of kisses has vanished,
    The tremblous lips, cold and still;
When the dream and the dreamer are banished,
    Shall we know of love's good or love's ill?

Was his soul of a saint or a sinner
    When men have forgotten to care,
Will Death or will Love be the winner
    Of the years of our passion and prayer?

ON WANSFELL PIKE   25

The hum of the bees midst the heather,
    The slumber of sheep in the brake;
The glory of sunniest weather,
    On the hills, on the tarn, on the lake.

The rush of the breezes blowing
    From summits afar in the west;
The murmuring mountain-brook flowing
    To the valley, as bird wings to nest.

The jet of a falcon's lost feather,
    Low fallen from loftiest flight,
On this glowing, velvety heather,
    Empurpled in afternoon light.

Over woods, over isles of Winander,
    Far south to the sands of the sea,
His reality, sweeter and grander
    Than the dreams of a dreamer may be.

O belovèd! O Nature, together!
    After years of estrangement, the sob
Of the loneliness stilled in the heather,
    While my heart upon thine is a-throb.

RHYMES OF THE BATTLEFIELD
To E.K.E., Yankton College

"Mere verse" to every friend beside,
  Mayhap some gentle thrill for you–
A vision of that Autumn-tide,
    When fresh from storied Waterloo,
      You clasped again my longing hand
      And both gave thanks for native land.

BEHIND THE LINES

"Here stood the –th New York Reserves
On July Third"– hard for the nerves
Of soldiers so to watch the charge
Of Pickett's line; their hearts grew large
With wish to hurl it down the hill.
Theirs, too, heroic soul and will
For he who offers nobly, serves.
Yea! mark their line–"the –th Reserves."

THE SHARP-SHOOTER

Deep down in this crevice of Devil's Den,
Whence, one by one he sought the men
Along the slope of yon Round Top,
Till a trembling vireo saw him drop,
The gray still wraps his nameless bones;
But gray of cold, unchiselled stones–
A silent mystery now as when
His firing ceased from Devil's Den.

SPANGLER'S SPRING 27

At night both drank from Spangler's Spring
With fevered thirst that battles bring.
They smiled at some poor soldier-joke,
A soldier's hope for peace awoke;
Brothers by weariness and night,
But foes when the summer dawn gave light.
The woods with maddened shouting ring
And blood steals down to Spangler's Spring.

BLUE-RIDGE

From yon dim haze the mountain-side
Shelters the valley far and wide–
"O mountains! in that battling throng
Which were in right, which were in wrong?"
Across the marble-shafted field,
Across the harvest's gathered yield,
'Tis thirty years and we abide;
Silent again is the mountain-side.

LINCOLN

On that long dead November day
As though one whispered *let us pray*
The silent circling patriots heard
The hero's humbly uttered word–
'Their deeds the world will keep, forget
Ere long the thoughts we speak,' and yet
The nation's heart shall cherish aye
Each word of that November day.

PEACE

We trace the sunken breast-work sod
Where with curse or prayer the soldier trod,
Waiting in awe that tide of gray
That swept the earth a mile away;
And gather amidst the ripened corn,
With a sob that fears nor doubt nor scorn,
These sprays of conquering golden-rod
Sprung from the sunken breast-work sod.

Gettysburg

QUESTIONING

Will the 'long, long years,' love,
    Teach my spirit how
It is 'better so,' love,
    Though I suffer now?

Is my life the richer,
    Knowing love through pain?
Though my soul is sadder,
    'Weakness to complain?'

Shall you never weary,
    Love, of the loveless home?
In some mood of longing
    Dream of those who roam?

His the child you cradle
    Sheltering on your breast;
Once–Shall you remember?–
    Mine its bliss and rest.

Is it 'better so,' love?
    Though I suffer now,
Will the 'long, long years,' love,
    Teach my spirit how?

THE PATH-MAKERS

When we first met,
We three,
The blades were knee-high in the cornfields.
When we last parted,
We three,
The wheat was stacked for the threshing,
The buckwheat gleamed in the moonlight,
The white-throated sparrows had vanished,
The frost was white on the grasses.

The location gang bequeathed us
Blueprints in a room above the store;
A broken line of wooden stakes,
Stretching ten miles
From the house of Widow Baker
On Maple Street,
Through oats and corn, through meadow, orchard,
Along the slough and up the hill
To Farmer Pitkin's yard
And snug beside his rusty barn;
Yes, bench-marks also,
To right and left of the broken line—
When one could find them.
We worked in calm and wind,
In sunshine and in thunder-storm
In heat that blistered flesh and whirled the brain.
The early morning saw us on our way,
And whippoorwills were fluting at our supper-time.

At night, all still below,   **31**
In the tiny upper chamber,
(Full of tobacco smoke and muttered cursing,)
We worked on estimates
Of areas and cubic contents
Of cut and fill,
Until the village clock tolled loud:
One–two–three–four–five–six–
Seven–eight–nine–ten–eleven–twelve.

And far afield,
Into hardened soil we wormed the rod
To find first shale and stone;
We waded the stream to mark the bridge
And we three tramped, tramped, tramped,
We three,
With axe and rod and level,
Along the tangent, around the curve,
In dust and mud and clay and thorny tangle,
Sweating, freezing,
Hungry, thirsting,
Cursing, praying,
Sometimes fagged and failing;
For we were the resident engineers
And the rails, the rails, were creeping close.

32

These too were ours:
Ripe plums in the shady orchard,
Cold water at Big Spring,
Noon rest beneath the wayside poplars!
Eggs in the meadowlark's nest,
The song of the indigo bunting
Through the August sultriness,
And the warble of vireo, bobolink, thrasher.

When we last parted,
We three,
When we last parted,
With "So long, boys,"
When we last parted, parting forever,
The frost was glistening on the rails
From Winona into Dover,
And the steam of Number One–
("Hurrah, boys, hurrah!")–
Soared white against the blue November sky.
Today they whirl along our path–
(With not a thought of us,
Us three, path-makers)–
The sallow banker to the surgeon,
The priest to his new parish,
The maiden to her wedding,
The sinner toward the Judgment Day,
And the unborn babe unto its birth.

Bertha May Booth 1896 [1893] 33

Grinnell's new president, John H.T. Main, spoke at
Bertha Booth's funeral in 1907. He had known Miss
Booth in his earliest years at the college, where he began
as a professor of Greek in 1892. Owing to poor health,
she was forced to interrupt her studies at Grinnell and
did not graduate until 1896. She was a brilliant young
woman, the valedictorian of her graduating class at
Anamosa High School, and later described as one of the
most intellectual students ever to attend Grinnell.
President Main was able to recall such things about her
as her membership in the "Morning-Glory Club," then
he reflected on how, during her continual struggle
against illness throughout her short life, she remained a
bright presence: "I think of her alone in Colorado,"
Main said, "disappointed, with the spectre of death
constantly before her, yet in spite of it all, cheerful
always."

   While at Grinnell, Bertha Booth worked on the
editorial staff of *The Unit*, the college's literary maga-
zine at that time, and regularly contributed poems to it.
She earned a diploma from the College of Oratory and
Physical Culture in Des Moines during her absence
from Grinnell, where she returned to graduate.
Subsequently her life appears to have been a quest in
search of health or at least a form of useful service
suited to her failing capacities. For a time she taught
school in Sutherland, Iowa, and in Grand Junction,
Colo.; but unable to sustain the rigors of regular public
school teaching, Bertha went to the Clarke School in
Northampton, Mass., to prepare herself for teaching

34   speech to the deaf. During those years she continued to
            write poetry—unpretentious and conventional but
            technically adroit and self-assured—and to publish it in
            The Unit. She died in Anamosa at the age of 36.

A DREAM

A road–walled, narrow, endless,–seemed.
　　Down it filed women, with gay speech,
In tears, in silence. From the stones
　　Sprung one red rose for each.

One plucked a branch,–in pain she cried:
　　"Ah–thorns! I'll suffer none of those!"
She snapped the stem off, flung it far,
　　And played toss with the rose.

Another tightly clasped her flower
　　In pale palms, stained and pierced and torn,
And smiling, while the blood dripped down,
　　She said: "Mine has no thorn."

36

HEAVENLY HEIGHTS
(To Sister Mary Josephine)

High on a mountain top a city gleamed,
 Girt round by walls of pearl, but not a trace
 Of the famed inner radiance of the place
Could I descry, although in song 'twas themed.
I bitter cried: "Mirage, thou has but seemed!"
 When lo, a gateway opened. Through its space
 Walked one, with glory shining in her face.–
And straight I knew the poets true had dreamed.
I cannot ask to enter in that gate;
 Mine eyes would be but blinded, and I know
  My heart too weak is for that rare, high air.
E'en this face–since Love regnant over fate,
 The city's gift, has kindled its calm glow–
  E'en this is pain. Too near I may not dare.

OPPORTUNITY   37

The Past man has bargained away
    For a mess of pottage bitter,
The Future he cannot buy
    Though mad with lust for its glitter.

The paltry and valueless Now
    Alone is his–prince he or peasant,
Yet black Past and gold-and-rose Future,
    Disguised, are the colorless Present.

INADEQUACY

How the cloud-folk of the sky
    Love the blue!
        Feel their being changing, torn,
        By their passion's tumult borne;
Yet their course in silence shy
    They pursue.

How the rocks that breast the sea
    Love the deep!
        Bare their bosoms to its beat,
        Joy both kiss and blow to greet,
Though they seem through rage or plea
    Sunk in sleep.

How the souls of us who plod
    Love the earth!
        Thrill at vales in sunrise light,
        Throb at mountains' cloud-girth might.
Dumb we gaze—then from our God
    Turn with mirth.

MOUNTAIN MIST   **39**

Across the hills she trails her ragged skirt–
  A maiden cloaked and veiled in clinging gray.
    In cruel mirth she clutches Sunshine's throat.
He writhes, escapes, and trembling, gasping, hurt,
    He seeks the smiling, gracious Plains remote.
  Then loves she him. She weeps her heart away.

40   TO A WATER LILY

O, pure priestess of the lake,
All a-quiver in the wake
  Of my boat,
When the blue-sheathed dragon flies,
Thine attendant votaries,
  Glance and float,
Hast thou never sighed to be
From thine altar-pads set free,
  Sighed to rise
Comrade of the zephyrs gay,
Sharing in their merry play,
  To the skies?

Helen Jean Bowen 1897   41

I've discovered very little about Helen Jean Bowen. Her
name appears on the staff and as a contributor to *The
Unit* during her undergraduate years at Grinnell, and
she must have been among the more promising of those
students whose interest in verse-writing was stimulated
and guided by Selden L. Whitcomb during his years on
the faculty around the turn of the century. Entries in
the Alumni Address Books for the years 1914 and 1918
indicate that she resided during that period in
Wellesley, Mass. Her occupation is given as "writer."

The only mature fruits of that occupation I have
gleaned are contained in a publication from the earliest
years following Helen Bowen's graduation from
Grinnell, a chapbook dated 1899 from the Wind-tryst
Press of Chicago and containing *Seven Sonnets*. A
slender product, but one that gives an authentic
glimpse of the literary manners and aspirations being
cultivated at places like Grinnell in the *fin de siecle*.

The interest of the poems themselves is augmented
by the existence of a review of Miss Bowen's *Seven Sonnets*
appearing in *The Unit* and written by Selden
Whitcomb himself. From that review one gains a vivid
sense of the kind of influence Whitcomb must have
been, the canons of taste he set before Grinnell
undergraduates. "The reader, jealous of the historical
nobility of the sonnet," Whitcomb remarks somewhat
prissily, "is glad to note that these are of the purest
Petrarchan type." He also marks Helen Jean's use of

42   "several melodious cadence rhymes" and suggests that
the appearance of assonance and alliteration "indicates
a musical instinct." Especially revealing—of both Miss
Bowen the apt pupil and Selden Whitcomb the
approving critic—are his comments on the language of
these sonnets: "the vocabulary is of definite poetic
beauty, including such words and phrases as *drapes,
mellow, ruddy, song-filled, brave control, vigil hour,
shivering grass* and *sad gray pinions.*" "These sonnets are
not final," Professor Whitcomb prudently adds,
"imperfections might easily be noticed. They are,
however, *vital*; artistically sincere in substance and
expression."

        That was Grinnell College in the "mauve decade,"
when everywhere—as Oscar Wilde wittily reminds
us—being earnest was of the highest importance.

SEVEN SONNETS   43

I

Mile upon mile the prairie's moonlit snow
Runs far to northward, far and bitter cold,
Fit vigil night! Another year is old,
And bitter yet the pain. Ah, long ago
I knew love first; still 'tis but pain I know!
Thrice to the New Year hath the twelve month rolled
With dragging wheel since my grieved heart hath tolled
Thy comings and thy goings, blow on blow.

Beloved, when another year hath passed,
Shalt thou be yet beyond the snowy miles
That stare at me and wonder at my grief?
Shalt thou have felt no faintest touch at last?
Are there for us no song-filled after-whiles
When these bare trees shall burst in bud and leaf?

44   II

Day breaks again. The ruddy sunrise cheer
Reddens the snow, and all through house and street
Is stir of living. Cheerily men greet
The dawning of another unknown year.
The vigil hour is past. The summons clear
Of common ties, of common duties meet
For daily living, of the bitter-sweet
Of sharing other's joy, strikes on my ear.

Beloved, though thou never turn to me,
Still I rejoice in loving thy strong soul,
Thy gentle, steadfast, patient, hero's heart.
May not each new-born year lead me to be
In some way worthy; heart in brave control,
To walk with thee, although long leagues apart?

IV   45

Love lies a-sleeping. After weary hours
Of strife and pain has fallen a quietude
Like unto death. No longer the mad mood
Of bitterness and longing overpowers
My spirit, and no longer my heart cowers
Before the world and hides in solitude.
A calm has come, a quiet interlude
Of peaceful fields and odorous poppy flowers.

I might dream love were dead, did I not know
Glance, clasp of hand, or sound of word of thine,
Of lilac or syringa-fragrance sweet
And memory-haunted, strain of music low
That once was known, would wake this love of mine
And teach my weary heart once more to beat.

46   V

May sun, and shade of youngling maple leaves
Across the lawns; the flitting of the jay
From dandelion to blossomed apple-spray;
Among the green elm buds the brown thrush weaves
A melody that winter's grief retrieves;
Through cherry-bloom the blue, not far away,
But near and yearning; while the breezes sway
The lilac buds thou lovedst in by-gone eves.

Beloved, all the miles that lie between
Us two breathe life and joy; earth's pulses stir,
And all her voices thrill with ecstasy.
We are her children; does our mother mean
For us no welling hopes, no wings a-whirr
Of strange, sweet visions we alone may see?

VI

The red rose of thy presence, radiant, rare
And royal, fills my soul with vibrant joy,
Unknown through all the weary months' annoy,
The days when sadness merged into despair.
Ah sweet with thee is all the summer air!
Thy name is all the blue-bird's songs' employ;
Thy nearness, as the warm spring rains destroy
The winter's ice, turns gloomy days to fair.

And yet thou turnest not thy golden heart
To me; thy beauty is all held concealed,
Save outer crimson petals closely furled,
And thy life's fragrance, which the winds impart
To every passer-by, who so is healed,
Unhealed am I alone of all the world!

48   VII

September sun shines on the purple grapes
The calm day long; the mellow apples hang
Reddening upon the quiet bough where sang
In May the ardent thrush; the spider drapes
Her shimmering web no errant fly escapes,
From branch to branch; the roadside sprang
But yesterday from green to gold that rang
Not, but in silence bloomed in flower shapes.

A benediction breathes from fruit and flowers
And sun and blue of sky. Ah, sweet is peace,
And sun and sky suffice the peaceful heart!
I crave no stormier love than is this hour's
When vagrant breezes' wooing brings me ease
And of our Mother's creatures I am part.

Joseph Walleser '03   **49**

Grinnell did not do entirely right by Joseph Garfield
Walleser. His connection with the college was extended
and highly creditable, but it took an unfortunate turn.

Joe Walleser came to Grinnell from Nashua, Iowa.
Evidently he made a strong mark as an undergraduate,
editing and writing for the literary magazine, singing in
the glee club, excelling in gymnastics, composing and
delivering the class ode at the graduation ceremony. He
was one of Professor John Main's prize students in
classical languages and went to Oxford in the first select
group of American students to win Rhodes Scholar-
ships. After three years at Oxford's Oriel College and a
brief stint teaching in North Dakota, Walleser was
brought back to Grinnell by John Main, who had
become president, and put in charge of courses in
English language and rhetoric. He seemed to have
settled easily and effectively into that role, but in
January 1925, the new literary magazine he had
founded (called *Junto*) imprudently published a
student's small-town exposé under the title "Blairsburg
Sketches." The names of Blairsburg citizens whose
peccadilloes these sketches revealed had carelessly been
left undisguised. Blairsburg was not amused, Grinnell
college was threatened with a libel suit, and President
Main put an end to *Junto* and to editor Joseph
Walleser's career at the college.

As a student, Walleser had composed a fight song
expressing predictable sentiments:

50

Forever true we'll stand by you,
In thick and thin we'll see you through,
Grinnell, Grinnell.

Sad to say, in a difficult moment Joe Walleser's college did not reciprocate; rather than seeing him through, it saw him off. He went on to teach high school in Cicero, Ill., and from there to Quincy College. He died in Chicago in 1959.

About writing Walleser was not personally ambitious; most of what he published appeared in his alma mater's literary magazines. But he is identified in a "Contributors" column in *The Tanager* (1933) as having "inspired more creative writing than any teacher before or since his time."

Walleser's own undergraduate poetry exhibits the late romanticism that Selden Whitcomb brought out in Grinnell writers of that generation. His more mature work continues to use the overblown diction, the emphatic rhythms, and the rapt posturing that came into favor with such English poets as Swinburne, Dowson, and Wilde. One hears, too, echoes of earlier Romantics like Shelley (in "The Eclipse") and Keats (in "To a Wren"). Like some of these illustrious predecessors, Walleser had traveled in the golden realms of classical Greek poetry; but apparently he turned a deaf ear to the brassy voices of his trailblazing contemporaries.

ON BEGINNING HOMER

As one sets out upon a journey, long
    Desired but never hoped to be, and turns
    His eyes about him questioning and learns
In truth his feet are bearing him along
With certain steps, yet holds his senses wrong
    And half believes some dream it is that burns
    Almost to being,–so my eye discerns
My Homer open, but I doubt the song.

For can it be that ever I may read
    This magic lore, and see and really know
        The great Achilles, touch him with my hand,
Or watch the swift-ensandalled Diomed?
    May I indeed with Priam's people go
        And sacrifice to her who guards the land?

THE ECLIPSE

Amid the strange-lit stars
    A shadow glows;
With weird dismay it mars
        The field of heaven and like a wizard knows
        And gloats that sorrow follows where he goes.

The moon has left her throne
    With veiled face
And mourns for what is gone.
        The dragon-darkness crawls into her place
        Robbing the night and her of her soft grace.

Late was she like a bride
    And calm as love
When love is satisfied,–
        When blending lips to timid passion prove
        Another heart wherein like raptures move.

A rose she was that spread
    Her beauty forth,
Peaceful at heart and fed
        With generous thanksgivings for her birth
        While she unknowing gave a joy to earth.

A moment was she bright,
    A moment fair,
Coming into the night
        And banishing the shades that gathered there;
        Now she is gone and night is everywhere;

Like dreams that proffer bliss
    We may not own–

A hope, a peace, a kiss,
    And ere they give, delay, and then are gone;
    And we return to old despair alone.

Lo, how her beauty lies!
    The rose is crushed;
The bride forsaken dies;
    The tints, the rays, the smiles with which she blushed
    Are rudely darkened and their praise is hushed.

Earth's forsaken meadows
    In darkness sleep
With unexpected shadows;
    The trees and rocks receive the gloom and keep
    Their unloved guest who lingers but to weep;

As when the wintered North
    Sees faintest morrow
Issue in azure forth
    And while a hope of Spring it dares to borrow
    Darkness returns like a deluded sorrow.

Like reason-guided minds
    The hills are hid,
Whose doubting only finds
    A darkness and a void unlimited
    Where once their humble gods a glory shed.

The glory falls and fades
    Through the black skies;
Darkness the dome pervades
    And sets the stars to weep their sympathies
    That they glow brighter with their tear-filled eyes;

54   As in the faithful Spring
         After cold snows
    When silenced robins sing,
         Over the ransomed fields the warm wind blows
         And flowers blossom when the winter goes.

         *   *   *   *   *   *   *

    Now from darkness bright'ning
         Light leaves the gloom;
    It flashes as of lightning
         The spirit moon and her enchantment come
         Transfigured from the dark and clammy tomb.

    Would that the lovely dreams
         Which illume Youth
    Might flood with radiant beams
         The night of aging Time as light endu'th
         The heavens now like a triumphant truth!

    Rebloom, white rose of heaven,
         Come forth, fair bride;
    That passing shadow was ever
         Like fear and envy, transitory; its pride
         Is spent; it hath endeared thee and hath died.

    Lo, in the lucid space
         She rideth by!
    Thou paragon of loveliness,
         So fair, thy beauty exiles memory,
         The dubious past expires when thou art nigh.

TO A WREN 55

Thou tiny, busy, modest-feathered sprite,
Prim as a matron in thy household cares,
What zeal is thine at work from morn till night
Bustling with a thousand hopes and fears!
Now scolding madly, now so filled with joy
That thou for very fulness wilt desist
And breaking into mazy melody
Quicken the air so blithe that all must list
And love thee, little cottage-seeking guest!

How winsome are thy pert, impulsive ways,
Thy smart, thy twittering activity,
Thy curious inquiry, and those lays
Sprung from thine ardency! I love to see
Thee come with Spring and seek the nooks and chinks,
The lease of which for years has been with thee,
And ere a watcher thinks
To find thee full-installed in thy neat privacy!

Amazing yet from childhood memories
Are songs of thine upon my window-ledge
Which faced the East and saw the morning skies.
A crevice in the casement's upper edge
Was thy conceded home for many years.
And every summer morning now it seems
I woke from happy dreams,
The sun upon my face, thy songs within my ears.

56
Fondly, sweet singer of a simple theme,
With every Spring thy song recalls
Those hours that slumber where no vision falls
But mine. I see as in a dream
A far-off child-deserted clime,
Its little share of sunny rays,
Its scenes and fancies blent in common days
Which live attended by a tender gleam
Of endless summer-time.
Thy singing summons it again;
By thy sweet strains I am re-born–
Sing on, and in thy gladness bright as then
Embalm for me that summer morn!

YOUTH
(From the French of Pascal-Bonetti)

My soul is like a dawn of April glittering,
　　Where nothing is but perfume, song and sunny sheen;
　　A thatched cottage leans there against a hillside green,
Shut to every perilous, windy, doubtful thing;
It is for my virginal lone dream's inhabiting.
　　Flower of stem impalpable, my heart in excess
　　Incenses it with odors, hope and giddiness.
My soul is like a dawn of April glittering.

I am like a rose where drinks the honey-bee,
　　So much song and odor in my heart is quickened,
　　And day after day, under suns too quickly dead,
My eyes, wonder-wide, are like baskets wherein be
Heavy fruits and leaves and flowers entwined wondrously.
　　Above them the bluebirds bewilderedly fly,
　　About them are dreaming the bright gardens of the sky.
I am like a rose where drinks the honey-bee.

I hold all the perfume of life in my hands,
　　My fair form's a garden of Hesperidean flowers,
　　I gather expectation from out the barren hours,
And the gold of days from among the trodden sands.
Proud and light-hearted, all the morrows I command.
　　My brow ringed with sunlight as with a rigol bound,
　　Like a child with a jewel with which he is astound
I hold all the gladness of life in my hands.

58

SUNSET
English version of Kroustallis's tribute to Epirus

I

The sun is kissing the summits goodbye,
And Heaven's rim—in thousands of hues,
Roseate greens and marigold blues—
Blurs where Hesperus claims the sky.

Chilling the heat of summer, a breeze
Descends from upland lake and river,
And drops the dews from old pine trees
With creaking of boughs and light-cone quiver.

The grass-bedded fountains sprinkle the flowers,
Murmuring, rocking them, bud and blade.
The Gulf turns gray, the dark cliff lowers,
The Zalungon blackens, the foothills fade…

And the valleys gloom to a green sea shade.

II

From soil newly broken the teamsters come,
Sunburnt and silent, worn and weary.
Heavy are the yokes and ploughs they carry…
And they urge their patient oxen home:–

"Ho-oh" is the shout, "Melissi! Lamberri!"
And the beasts plod on, with occasional lowing,
Their horns like wreathes and half-moons showing.

Out of the byways women come, carrying
Various burdens…..Strong-limbed, bold,
At any stump pausing, at any tree tarrying,
They wipe their sweat on an apron's fold.

Cheerful and sweet are the words they say,
Under the trees, at the close of the day:–

"Ours is a world of health and joy!"

III
Shy as a fawn, the shepherd boy
Whistles to keep his flock in pace,
And leads them down from foothill to folding–
With how many trials!–to the milking place.

Nearby he hears a goatherd, scolding
A flock of mischievous goats–that goes
With many more trials than a shepherd boy knows!

"Tsup-tsup! Oh-ee!" the goatherd yells,
While nannies and billies elude his blows
With mocking bleats and jingle of bells.

Far off–the notes of a flute are heard,
And the boom of the gun of a hunter or guard.
The echoes in one hoarse song are shut
By the singing groom near the breeder's hut.

60

IV

The valley's wild birds congregate,
With enormous chatter, to roost in the wood.
The johnny-bird mourns his dead brother's
        fate.
The owl hoots in her solitude.

Water-turtles with eager throats are vying.

The nightingale hides in the bramble grove
To sing in his rhythm his song of love.

The wizard bat, in crazy flight,
Zigzags across the depths of night,

Teasing the farmer's boy with its flying.

V

Oh! dear, dear life of my homeland and town,
Where paths are plain and rewards are clear,
Dear are your ways, and of all, most dear,–
Your returning home when the sun goes down!

James Norman Hall '10

Anyone curious about extraordinary people who
attended Grinnell College should straightaway read *My
Island Home*, the autobiography James Norman Hall
had not quite completed when he died in 1951.
"Norman," "Jim," or "Jimmy" (depending on the time
and place) tells in that book of growing up in Colfax,
Iowa, and of sometimes riding on the cowcatcher of the
eastbound train to jump off at nearby Grinnell, where
he would roam the streets of that romantic town,
marveling at the big clapboard houses gleaming in the
moonlight and the sounds of the college glee club
wafting through the soft spring night. He later attended
that college and sang in that glee club, writing the
words and music for "Sons of Old Grinnell," a school
song some of us were required to learn by heart and are
unable to forget.

Hall was a romantic, but an earnest one, and his
whole life was an adventure that deserves to be read in
detail. Having gone to England in 1914 to devote
himself to writing, he volunteered in the British army
when war with Germany broke out and wrote a book
about that experience called *Kitchener's Mob*. After
Corporal Jimmy Hall was discharged from his infantry
battalion so he could visit his ailing father, he returned
to France, joined the Lafayette Escadrille, learned to fly
pursuit planes, and became a flight commander before
he was shot down and imprisoned in Germany.

After the Great War, Hall met a fellow pilot named

62 Charles Nordhoff, and the two collaborated in writing an official history of the Lafayette Flying Corps. But that was only the beginning of their careers as co-authors. The two went to Tahiti, pursued their separate lives as writers, but eventually became world famous as the authors of *Mutiny on the Bounty* and its two sequels, *Men Against the Sea* and *Pitcairn's Island.*

A dreamily unassuming and sweet-natured man, Hall loved the work of Robert Louis Stevenson and Joseph Conrad; but he also harks back to Emerson and Thoreau. Experiencing war and then living in remote Tahiti, he came to loathe modernity, but never his native Iowa. Known best as a writer of prose romance, Norman's deepest and most abiding sense of himself was as a poet. He seems to me wonderfully gifted and fluent as a writer of light verse, a kind of inspired and entirely unpretentious doggerel. This talent found its fullest expression in that charming, surprisingly poignant, and side-splittingly comic literary hoax, *Oh Millersville!* This is a collection of poems purported to have been written by a small-town Iowa girl of between 9 and 11 years old named "Fern Gravel." Hall published them under Fern's name in 1940 and thoroughly relished his deception. Some of the poems in *Oh Millersville!* have been made into an extremely successful song cycle by composer Jon Chenette of Grinnell's music faculty.

I could not resist representing Hall's poetry by three examples of Fern Gravel's work along with a selection from his more straightforward poems.

THE ATTACK

Two days and nights a storm of shell
Had rocked the earth. Then silence fell.

The very hills were beaten down
With mines, and where had stood a town
But half in ruin–scarce a stone
Remained to show there had been one.

We stumbled along, knee-deep in mire,
Through shell-holes, ditches, tangled wire,
And slithered into a first-line trench
Filled with dead men and lyddite stench.

Not a sound in that grim place;
Not a living foe to face;
And we could only stand and stare,
Hardly believing we were there.

Then came our turn to wait until
The enemy had *his* chance to kill
From gun positions miles away;
And so we waited all that day;

And so we waited through the night,
Shoveling bodies out of sight,
For underfoot and over head
Lay the hateful happy dead.

But what I best remember, came
During *our* bath of steel and flame:
The German dead were killed again

64

With scores and hundreds of our men—
But let this be: no words could tell
How such things were, or what befell.

There came a lull. A hush spread round
Louder than any loudest sound.

Six of us, crouching close in mud
That was part water and part blood,
Looked up, and our Irish sergeant said:
"Cheer up lads! We ain't *all* dead!

"Blimy!" he added, "for all that mill
There's an Irish flag a-wavin' still!"

On the edge of our shell-hole parapet,
Lined in airy silhouette
Against a sky of white and blue
A single cluster of green grass grew.

We looked and smiled and looked again,
We six shell-bewildered men—
There were but two of us at last,
But all day long our "flag" stood fast.

Never, I think, had kindly Spring
Done a more kindly, needful thing
Than when she set her banner there.
How blithely it waved in the morning air!

It seemed an answer to the roar
Of all the bellowing mouths of War.

NEW YORK   **65**

I. One Autumn Afternoon

Seen from afar, at the golden end of day,
Taking the westering sun in points of light,
It seemed a city built in Death's despite,
Builded to music, as old legends say
Camelot was; a city where decay
Comes not, nor evil chance, nor any blight
To men's high hopes. Oh, glorious the sight
I saw that afternoon from far away.

But later, in the evening, in the murk,
Were gusty, rain-drenched streets and squares beset
With old realities in ancient kind:
Drabs and beggars, the maimed and halt and blind;
Penniless men on benches, cold and wet;
Tired charwomen going home from work.

II. From My Room In East 70th St.

All I could see was just his hands
Framed in an attic window-square,
Shuffling cards and laying them out;
Someone playing solitaire.

A brick-paved court was in between
My window and his own. I read
All afternoon, and still he played.
At midnight when I went to bed

66

His lighted window showed the hands
At their old game of working through
The pack. New York's a lonely place
For some old men—and young ones, too.

III. The Bread Line

The thing that numbs the heart is this:
That men cannot devise
Some scheme of life to banish fear
That lurks in most men's eyes.

Fear of the lack of shelter, food,
And fire for winter's cold;
Fear of their children: lacking these...
This is a world so old,

Where men have lived so long, so long,
Finding no way to share
The bounty of a world so rich
That none need suffer there.

THE JOURNEY TO COME

Millersville, oh, Millersville!
That is my home and I like it, but still
I wish that once in a while I could go
To cities like Omaha and St. Jo.
You get tired of living in such a small town
With so few streets for walking around.
I would like to visit some larger places
And see many thousands of different faces
Of people I do not know at all
That you cannot see in a town so small.
But I wouldn't want to go for good;
Just for a while, and then I would
Want to come back to Millersville,
Because I love my home and I hope I always will.
But I love trains better than everything;
I would rather travel than anything.
Next summer I am going nearly out of this state,
To Keokuk; I can hardly wait,
On the Mississippi river. We will stay two days.
It will be the first time I have been such a ways
From Millersville. I hate to come home
So soon, but I guess we will have to come.
The convention my father is going to
Is only for that long, and when it is through
He must come straight back to his business here,
And I'll have to stay home all the rest of the year.

  —"Fern Gravel"

POETRY

Of all our American poetry
I like Longfellow's the best.
It makes me cry to read them;
They are better than the rest.

Some of James Whitcomb Riley's
Are as silly as can be.
How a grown-up man could write them
Is a mistery to me.

Whittier's *Snowbound* is a poem
That is very very fine.
I have read it more than a dozen times,
Every single line.

I am going to write poems
To make other people cry;
I expect to finish thousands
Before I have to die.

Sometimes in a single day
I have finished three.
Today I have done just this one
Which is beautiful to me,

And it says just what I think
Of some poetry I have read.
James Whitcomb Riley is still living.
The other two are dead.

–"Fern Gravel"

THE OVER-NIGHT GUESTS

The Iowa College glee club
From the town of Grinnell
Gave a concert here this week.
Everyone liked it so well.

We all went to it,
And farmers came from many miles.
The church was so crowded
They had chairs in the aisles.

There were twelve songs on the program
But they sang many more.
For every one they sang
They had to give an encore.

There were no more trains that night
So the glee-club had to stay
In different people's houses
Until the next day.

Two came to our house.
They were very polite.
They wore swallowtail suits
And their ties were white.

We have one spare-room
And that was theirs.
They ate some apple-pie and milk
And then they came upstairs.

70

One of them asked my father,
"Where is your bathroom, please?"
And he had to tell them
We didn't have one of these.

I was so ashamed
I shut my door quick.
Not to have a bathroom
Nearly makes me sick.

I hope we never have anyone
Stay at our house again
Until we do have one.
Especially, college men.

There ought to be one
In all the Millersville houses.
So far there are only two,
At the Dodd's and the Smouse's.

—"Fern Gravel"

Ruth Suckow '14   71

She was the daughter of a Congregational minister
whose succession of pastorates sound like the entries in
an Iowa Girls' Basketball Tournament or some crazily
roundabout itinerary for RAGBRAI (the [Des Moines]
Register's Annual Great Bike Ride Across Iowa):
Hawarden, LeMars, Algona, Fort Dodge, Manchester,
Davenport, Grinnell. With that kind of exposure to the
warp and woof of life in the Midwest, is it any wonder
that Ruth Suckow's stories and novels made her one of
that region's most important writers from the mid-
1920s until her death in 1960?

Though Ruth transferred from Grinnell College in
1913, she had graduated from Grinnell High School
and her knowledge of both town and campus is
manifest in the early novella *A Part of the Institution.*
"Professor Wilder," a minor character in *The Bonney
Family*, is a fictionalized version of her literature teacher
Joseph Walleser [pp. 49–60], whose class in lyric poetry
she remembered fondly. ("He doesn't make you pick
out metaphors and that darned old central thought,"
Suckow's character Sarah Bonney admiringly exclaims.)
As it happened, lyric poems were Ruth's own initial
form of literary expression. She published poetry in
both *Touchstone* and *The Midland* in 1918, and three
years later a group of her short poems appeared in
Poetry. One of these, "Beauty," makes clear (at least in
retrospect) that Ruth Suckow was already headed along
the path of those writers who saw realism as the style

72

and narrative fiction as the form that would distinguish
American literature in the 20th century:

Beauty I found then
In eyes, and in the strange
Twisted lives of men.

SONG IN OCTOBER

Heart, as shiningly wear your grief
As frost upon a lilac leaf;
As mist along the stubble rye,
As silver rain across the sky.

PRAYER AT TIMBER-LINE

Oh, that I could fashion words
    As the wind bends the trees–
Could shape my lines as shining-bare,
    As exquisite, as these
White branches of the writhen pine
Standing alone at timber-line!

Winds of life, blow stinging-free
    Into my heart that's waiting, still!
Beat on my words unceasingly,
    And shape them to your stern white will!

BEAUTY

I went where pines grew;
    Beauty I found in these,
In stars, and in the strange
    Twisted boughs of trees.

I went where houses were;
    Beauty I found then
In eyes, and in the strange
    Twisted lives of men.

THE ODD ONES

I like best those crotchety ones
    That follow their own way
In whimsical oblivion
    Of what the neighbors say.

They grow more rare as they grow old,
    Their lives show in their faces–
In little slants and twisted lines;
    Like trees in lonely places.

GRAMPA SCHULER

Grampa Schuler, when he was young,
Had a crest of hair, and shining eyes.
He wore red-flowered waistcoats,
Wild Byronic ties.
The whole land of Germany
Wasn't wide enough!–
He ran away one night, when winter
Seas were fierce and rough.

He has a sleek farm here
With already a settled air.
He's patriarchal, with his sons
And daughters round him everywhere,
His son's son Jim has fiery eyes–
He wants to go where the land is new!
Grampa bitterly wonders: "What are
Young fools coming to!"

78   *Verna Grubbs '16*

Writing under the pen name "Ann Winslow," Verna
Grubbs published poetry in *Contemporary Vision*,
Contemporary Verse, and *The Harp*. In 1931 a spate of
her poems appeared in several issues of Grinnell's
Tanager. At that time that literary magazine had a solid,
if limited, national reputation that made it considerably
more than an outlet for student work. Verna Grubbs
was then assistant professor of speech at Grinnell
College. She left the college in 1935 and made her
home in Laramie, Wyo., as Ann Winslow.

POEMS I

CAPRICE–

A grotesque tree and a wind at will,
A sodden sun on a yellow hill,
Grey smoke blankets hung out for an airing:

These are mine for the faring
From my back stoop to the next in weather
That sulks like a child with lips together.

NEW MOON

Atalanta is paring the golden apple
And tossing the rinds to the sky,
The fruits of Hippomenes dropped on the path
As he went swiftly by.

One scimitar segment has pierced the clouds
And rides in the purpling blue
That dyes the mantle of evening
Before the stars cut through.

SECOND SPRING

There is such a thing as a new shoot springing
From an old and withered bough,
There is such a thing as a new love bringing
Joy to a heart dead now.

So do not weep and gather petals
Fallen after the rain:
New white love does not break to blossom
Without some pain.

POEMS II

ROMANTICISM

Days of mad yearning,
Then my hunger satisfied.
Craving is over.

I hold it loosely
And my tongue cleaves mute; the thing
is not what I sought.

LANTERNS AT DUSK

A beacon of light
Flares upon the deepening sky.
(Pale phosphorescence)

Here another gleam
As gray evening scatters day.
(Shy blushing firefly)

VAIN LONGINGS

You are not mine now.
I chide the day to return
That old love of you.

RENDEZVOUS

Silence over the brooding town,
Dusk on the campus hill,
My heart is beating softly
Where the road stands still.

Where the road is standing still,
Broken the field and mellow;
Through haunted willow boughs
The moon shines yellow.

I must turn and walk again
Homeward to my sorrow,
Drug my soul in heavy sleep
Until this hour tomorrow.

82   *Grace Hunter '17*

A native of Wapello, Iowa, Grace Eva Hunter was a
member of Grinnell College's English department from
1927 until 1963. She earned M.A. and Ph.D. degrees
from the University of Iowa and, before joining
Grinnell's faculty, taught in the public schools in
Wapello, Marengo, Fort Dodge, and Tulsa, Okla.

Honors and distinctions came her way—Grace was
a president of the Grinnell chapter of Phi Beta Kappa
and of the Iowa Poetry Society, she was an editor of
Grinnell's literary magazine *The Tanager*, and in 1952
she received a Grinnell College Alumni Award—but
she was not one to make much noise about her wide
interests and considerable accomplishments. These
included published translations of Swedish poetry as
well as the appearance of her own poems in magazines
and journals, including the *American Mercury*. Her
experience in the schools of Iowa and Oklahoma in her
early years contributed to her deep concern with
poverty; she lectured on that subject at workshops and
writers' conferences.

PHEASANTS

Ironweed above them,
Blue ditch below,
A dozen pheasants
Basked in the snow.

Like birds of bronze,
Each in his place
Took the great noon
And all the sun's grace;

Or like men at devotion
Sculptured in stone,
Safe from the arrow
And sword at the bone.

Metallic luster
Clanged in the snowfield,
Still in the stillness
Of loveliness sealed.

Oh, swift come the darkness
Of transcendent flight;
But slow be the moment
Meridian bright.

JUNE NIGHTS

Two spires of yucca bloom beside the door
Of her neat bungalow; a well-pruned vine
Makes frugal shadow all along the floor.
In her prim garden in the morning shine
She takes a walk with steps precise and slow.
When she could have a child, she had no child.
And she was widowed a long time ago;
No wonder she is virginal and mild,
And cannot understand the gaiety
Of laughing girls when every joyous air
That titillates the dainty poplar tree
Is fingering their warm breasts and lips and hair.
June nights what can she know of youth's queer craze
When yucca flowers pale by dark doorways.

RELEASE

Let us walk in the sun:
Too long has inflexible shade
Of dead columns and walls,
Steel and stone, chilled and made us afraid.

For a vista of light
Let us hollow out time and space
And with living trees
Make metamorphic shapes of our grace.

In the seamless air
By a stream on a globe ever turning,
Let us walk, let us run
In the face of the sun, burning and burning.

86   SOUTHERN PACIFIC: GOLDEN TRUMPET

Morning in New Mexico
rears bold rosy rocks
at the rim of flat land
cactus-sown and strange
in the blue gloom
of a rainy autumn sky.

Afternoon in Texas
stretches a long sapphire cloud
over miles of level loneliness.

Evening in Kansas
televises white prodigious granaries
while the wide dusk slowly, slowly
veils windmills,
the brown backs of Herefords and horses,
and a single tree of cloud on the horizon.
The highway, fringed with sunflowers,
flows backward faster and faster
as the earth turns,
and the train, rushing to midnight and morning,
trumpets the dark questing note of speed.

Evelyn Mae Boyd '18 87

After graduating from Grinnell and going on to Columbia University, "Evie" Boyd returned to her alma mater to teach medieval literature and a variety of writing courses over a long career that spanned four decades. She spent the academic year 1926–27 on leave from Grinnell teaching at Kobe College in Japan—and acquiring a taste for Japanese art that remained a significant part of her sensibility. She was absent from the college during much of World War II while serving overseas with the American Red Cross. Upon her retirement from Grinnell, Evie continued teaching at Waterloo University in Ontario, Canada, where she was faculty adviser to the literary magazine *Ciaroscuro*. Though a devoted medievalist (including particularly but by no means exclusively Chaucer and Dante), her literary enthusiasms ranged widely, from Pre-Raphaelite poetry to the modern theatre. She was a co-editor with Grinnell's Paul Spencer Wood of the popular "survey anthology" *Masters of English Literature*. A collection of her writings, *The Lure of Creatures True and Legendary*, was published in Canada in 1978.

Though her own sense of literature as an academic subject often seemed caught up in the distant and even the arcane, Evelyn Boyd was always down-to-earth in her encouragement and support for any and all earnest literary efforts on the part of her students. In my experience, she was ever encouraging and almost never satisfied. Beneath that breathless excitement was the

88   stickler who opened one's eyes to the fact that writing
          proceeds, and so must satisfy us, one word at a time.
          She saw it as a matter of infinite choices, none of which
          should go uninterrogated.

LINES

Sorrow like a seedling tree
Long ago took root in me

Fed upon my days and years
Drank for nurture all my tears

Traced its dark boughs through my heart
Stripping life and love apart

Held me when I would have pray'd
Mute in an embrace of shade.

It covers with its leaves my soul
Murmuring in their depths my dole

Weighs my eye-lids down with dark
Stills my ears to song of lark

With its hunger stops my breath
Chills me with the thought of death

From my frenzy draws its calm,
From my anguish gathers balm.

– May Lee (pseud. for Evelyn Mae Boyd)

ST. COLUMB'S EVE

The angels in the moon-rise sing, O soft, o'er sweet Derry,
Thirty thousand angels singing praise to Columb's memory,
With *laudamus* to Cuchulain, *benedicite* to Bride,
O'er the little town of Derry shining white on Aran's side.

The music in the moon-rise mingles down upon the shade
Of fox-glove in the meadow and heather in the glade,
And the red-eared fawns start fearless in the drifting of the song
And the sainted unseen Columb smiles o'er Derry all night long.

– May Lee (pseud. for Evelyn Mae Boyd)

SEA GRIEF   **91**

What matters the clean-swept floor, my mother,
The polished glass on the board,
Our only guest is dull sorrow's brother
And his children, a blinded horde.

What matters our sheep in the acre,
Our corn in the back hills beyond,
The white thorn knots for our Sunday hearth,
The turfs piled high in a mound.

The sea through the fog is keening, my mother,
The sea that was tender–and harsh,
We'll gaze through the mists with our guest, sorrow's brother,
And hear the wind roar in the marsh.

– May Lee (pseud. for Evelyn Mae Boyd)

MAPLE LEAVES

ARASHIYAMA

The shaded path is stained with scarlet
And beneath the bridge of Niyaku-oji
The waters from Arashiyama flow quietly.
The maples bend across the stream;
Their red leaves falling cover the white stones on the bottom.

MIDERA

Combed into a formal pattern
Lie the white sands of the temple courtyard.
The chant of the Buddhist mass
Rises, falls—rises, falls,
Sacredly, ceaselessly, in dirge-like rhythm.
Drum and bell—drum and bell.
Upon the black-lacquered floor
Scarlet maple leaves sink their deep color,
As in the clear and quiet waters of Kyoto.

John C. Kemmerer '23 93

The arts of writing and printing were early interests of John Kemmerer as he grew up on a farm in Guthrie County, Iowa, and they remained consuming avocations throughout his life. At Grinnell, he concentrated on English and history, served on the staffs of the humor magazine, *The Malteaser,* and the yearbook, *The Cyclone,* wrote poetry for *The Unit,* worked as a printer's devil at the local newspaper, and was elected to Phi Beta Kappa. After earning a master's degree at Harvard, he taught English for a year at Northwestern then studied at Columbia University while writing stories, plays, a novel, and poetry.

In 1929 John married Ruth Chamberlain '22, a fellow Grinnellian, and the following year began working for a consulting engineering firm in New York City. During the 1930s, he was studying typography in night courses at New York University, building his own hand press, and beginning to publish his own books. Finally in 1950 John bought a farmhouse in Connecticut where he located his presses. Thereafter, much of his time was taken up publishing limited editions of his own poetry and an autobiographical sketch. One volume of his poems, *The Wild Plum Tree,* was published by the Prairie Press in Iowa City.

John Kemmerer's work is that of a strongly independent-minded person living his life, as Thoreau recommended, "deliberately"—pursuing his interests, observing his surroundings, following his own bent.

94

The result is pleasing, well-turned, concise verse. His poems show some of Frost's directness and perhaps a touch of the teasingly noncommittal particularity of William Carlos Williams—except more songlike and, it seems clear to me, with none of the sheer cheek of someone able, like Dr. Williams, to change the history of poetry.

SPRING IN WINTER

Raccoon river's bluest water
Flashes under hills of snow,
Like old Henry's lovely daughter,
Spring in winter, yes and no.

THE WILD PLUM TREE

Loud sings the meadowlark
In the sparkling dew;
White the wild plum tree
Blooms by the mill.

Green grow the woods
In the midday sun;
The river rolls foaming
Over the dam.

Now sings the lover
"I love you;"
Bright the moon shines
On the midnight hill.

ECHO

The country boy who in late afternoon
Calls the cattle in, *Come boss, come boss,*
Idles, and hears his echo at the barn,
A person wondering and crying *Boss.*
No more than his unlettered herd, or some
Grasshopper in the lane, does he suppose
That once in Argos by the setting sun
For other boys the word for cows was BOES.
But still he calls, and still the cattle come.

WILD PRAIRIE THEN

Wild prairie then
To the young rider;
No house, not a tree,
Only the green waves
And the horizon;
As it seemed to him,
No land in sight,
Only *one vast sea.*

BLACKBERRIES

Blackberries are a roving tribe,
Rowdy Vikings were not wilder;
They appear, land anywhere,
Leap to flourishing invasion,
Big leaves, thickets, long sharp thorns,
Sometimes a berry that is sweet,
Then they droop and disappear;
Local weeds at once replace them.

100   FOUR EPIGRAMS

ICARUS

Vain was your flying, Icarus, lifting
        Thin wings of wax toward the sun;
Vain your fable: today we fall by fifties,
        And think our flight has just begun.

NOVICE REPROVED

He would not dare to say that *you* are *thou*;
Such a thing his peers do not allow.
Leave that to Omar underneath a bough,
Be new, they say, be violent, be now.

WHERE THE SNOWS ARE

When foggily the painter sighed,
"*Where are the snows of yesteryear?*"
All the slender girls replied,
"Here," and again, "we're here, we're here."

NIGHT WEATHER

Moonlight for the highwayman,
Or the white moon on the sea,
But for lovers a nightlong rain.

Roma Kauffman '26

During her student years, Roma Kauffman was a mainstay of Grinnell's literary magazines. She published work (poems, fiction, and a play) in both *Verse and Fiction* and its longer-lived successor *The Tanager*. Twice, in 1924 and again in 1925, she won the annual poetry prize and was one of the first student editors of *The Tanager*. After graduation, Roma Kauffman worked in the college's public relations department and remained at Grinnell until the mid-'30s, occasionally publishing in *The Tanager*, whose reputation flourished as it attracted contributors and a readership beyond the campus.

102   GARDEN PATHS

The night like lavender-dust is sifting
    Through the soft meshes of the trees.
Above the box-hedge, mists are lifting.

The crickets strike up melodies
    They played a hundred years ago
In sanded garden paths like these.

Alyssum, like forgotten snow,
    Drifts near the bench, where talk sometimes
The ghosts of lovers, soft and slow.

And where the mauve wisteria climbs,
They flirt and love in pantomimes.

POEMS–TWO FAREWELLS   **103**

QUENCH THE TORCH

Quench the torch now. Plunge it deep and quickly
Into the still, cold waters of the mind,
Never again to lift its leaping radiance.
But go now, quiet, resolutely blind

To any after-image. Let us summon
Wills to unloose taunt nerves and muscles tense,
Walk slowly, head high, into choking darkness.
Quench the torch now, and quietly go hence.

SYMPHONY IN TWO MOVEMENTS
(Dated respectively December and February)

Lugubrioso
Deep to the bone these iron links have bitten
That bind my flesh against you, year by year.
Unalterable now the law seems written
That fetters only grow to me more dear.

Allegretto
Mere brittle, hygienic glass the things
Do prove, that once my faithful flesh corroded.
O, let the galled jade wince, my heart now sings!
For fetters, ex-my-love, are long outmoded.

104   *Augusta Towner Reid '28*

As Loren Reid '27 nimbly puts it in his biographical
summary at the conclusion of his wife's *Poems and Verses*
(1997), "At Grinnell she majored in English, swim-
ming, basketball, tennis, partying, chapel, grading
papers, and tending the music library, graduating with a
Phi Beta Kappa and a husband." Gus Reid, as every-
body calls her, has led an avidly varied and accom-
plished life, in which verse writing has played a
considerable part. Educated in the Des Moines schools,
Grinnell College, the University of Iowa, and the
University of Missouri, she can claim eminent mentors:
John P. Ryan in speech, Hardin Craig in Shakespeare,
and John G. Neihardt in writing. Her long career in
teaching in high school and college includes an
impressive range of subjects: speech, English, world
history, general science, and basketball. At her retire-
ment she was teaching composition and rhetoric at the
University of Missouri; she is a charter member of the
Columbia chapter of the Missouri Writers' Guild.

Augusta Reid unabashedly associates herself with
"an earlier school" of poetry, "in which music and
rhyme were obvious, not to mention … ideas." Her
engagingly unpretentious and sure-handed work has
appeared in *The Saturday Evening Post, Ave Maria,
Science* and *Scientific Monthly*. Warning that "poets [are]
not completely sane on self-evaluation," she acknowl-
edges a partiality to "the music-filled rollicking ones"
among her own poems.

CHILD ON A HILL　　　　　　　　**105**

Up the far hill he runs,
　　Vagrantly as a blown leaf,
　　　　A distant vibrancy stirring the grasses.
Stopped at the farthest crest,
　　Arm-deep in mullein stalks,
　　　　He lingers; finds, beyond our sight,
Some long enchantment blooming
　　In that far sky.

Tiny, remote... alone.
　　No longer, even in grief,
　　　　Can he be ours, but pledged to passes
Far and strange. And we–
　　We know the future walks,
　　　　Surer than faith, beyond our sight.
With love our only gift
　　For that far sky.

THE FAERY SNOW

The turned-up pail with a cushion on it,
　　Trees with pillows in their laps,
A fence post with a furry bonnet,
　　And bushes wooly in their wraps

Have touched my brain and turned my senses
　　By some witchery of scene;
I'll snatch a collar from the fences
　　And reign in ermine as a queen.

OCTOBER MIDNIGHT

No flickering stars relight among the grasses,
    No great cicadas trill;
The dark and velvet warmth of summer passes,
    For nights are blue and chill.

The coldly rushing air swings on the willows,
    And suddenly is fled;
The scattering acorns, blown in gusty billows,
    Strike sharply overhead.

108

PIONEERS

(on reading Rölvaag's *Giants in the Earth*)

From out the land of earth and sky they came,
    And vanished at the line where sky meets earth,
Time has no hours, and day itself no name
    Where are but light and dark in slow rebirth.
The thin curve of a guide rope in the grass
    Is set against the sky's immensity,
And on the prairie's silent, billowing mass
    The covered wagons seek their destiny.

Spare bodies, aching for the night's hard ease;
    Shy souls, that loneliness has set apart;
        Strong wills, to sow the future from their palm,
What greatness lay unseen, that men like these
        Dared match the boundless heavens with their hearts,
        And ever-widening prairies with their calm?

PORTRAIT

–And still she talked, still bred the foundling words:
    Inconsequential waifs, homeless and lost
To the great arch of thought–small quivering birds
    In aimless flutter on her footless breath–
Like dead leaves swirling in a hollow tree,
    Caught by the bitter wind of past Novembers.

–Beneath this antic aimlessness, the sense
    Of hapless hollows and amorphous hells
That hatch such changelings. Here the impotence
    Of hopeless heart repacing hopelessness,
Of limp despair, and mindless need, that be
    The bitten buds of things her heart remembers.

THE SEARCHING HEART

All roads lead out for a child
Like spokes for the axled heart–
The whir of their turning an unuttered yearning,
            "Depart!"

A roadway brushes the sky
The wilderness is a song,
Where wild things quicken, the wonder-stricken
            Belong.

The faraway place of the stars,
That bends to the reaching mind,
Is his to be given, because he is driven
            To find.

Small furry things of the field,
And the soft, gray mourning dove–
Of these he is heedful, because it is needful,
            To love.

All roads lead out to the sky,
And, trying its curving dome,
He yields to the yearning of all things returning
            Home.

Harry Duncan '38

Although best known as a printer at the forefront of the
American private-press movement in the latter half of
the 20th century, Harry Duncan was also a poet whose
work had its moment of strong critical acclaim. Born in
Keokuk, Iowa, he majored in English at Grinnell and
went on to graduate study in that subject at Duke
University. While working at the Cummington School
in Massachusetts, Duncan discovered the joys and
demands of high-quality printing, and in association
with Katherine Frazier and Wightman Williams he
helped to make the Cummington Press one of the very
finest small presses in the country. After the deaths of
both Frazier and Williams, Harry Duncan returned to
the Midwest to teach printing at the University of Iowa
and then at the University of Nebraska at Omaha. The
Cummington Press continued in operation, and
Duncan also printed books under the Abbatoir Press
imprint. He is especially associated with the production
of books of poetry by some of the most important
American writers of his time: Wallace Stevens, Robert
Lowell, and James Merrill. At his death in 1997,
Duncan had attained an extraordinary reputation
among small-press printers for his meticulous crafts-
manship and his uncompromising regard for the finest
materials.

If Harry Duncan's devotion to printing eclipsed his
own achievement as a poet, he nonetheless attracted the
attention of some in whose judgment he stood among

112   the most gifted poets of his generation. In 1954 Charles
Scribner's Sons published a volume in its *Poets of Today*
series that included a substantial body of work from
three younger poets: Harry Duncan, Murray Noss, and
May Swenson. The volume featured a critical introduc-
tion by John Hall Wheelock. That distinguished
American poet and editor was outspoken in his
admiration for Duncan's contribution, which along
with original poetry included translations of Dante,
Beaudelaire, Rilke, and Apollinaire. Describing Harry
Duncan as "a modern in the line of the 17th-century
metaphysicians," Wheelock praised his "restrained
intensity," which on occasion vents itself, according to
this critic, "in sarcasm and satire, in a bitterness or a
disgust, violent and disillusioned." "This," remarked
Wheelock, "is the other side of strong feeling; it is the
obverse, also, of [Duncan's] delicate lyricism."

A BUGLER, DYING

Sir, all the field lies mown
    and now the loud machines
    are stopped, than grass cut down
    less murmurous. Such peace
    leaves generals alone
    to pace their open grave
    naming the numberless
    whose battles brace the brave
    and hearing them converse
    when twilight intervenes,
    rapt garlands of the dead
    on the air faint and terse
    to rattle a vaulted head
    and cleanse the spendthrift pod,
    milkweed and goldenrod,
    clover and timothy–
    enfranchised poverty
    first learned at Mother's knee.
    And the spilled seed is God.

114   EAST ROCK

Sharp shadows lined the bricky, sun-paled rocks,
    but long ago our sires had scared away
    all bears and braves along the trail they'd blazed,
    no peril seemed that lax forenoon when we
    climbed up the cliff-face in their wake and gazed
    from where sightseeing flocks
    had even raised a fence and splashed red paint
    to warn of Dangerous Height, in fear that falling
    might follow so steep a downward look, feeling
    heady towards heaven where world spreads far and faint.
Behind us, trees were tufted sprigs with black
    ink-spatters under them, cars, routine ants,
    the wry creek, a crack in porcelain park;
    and Lilliputian from our eminence,
    compact and clean as whittled Noah's Ark
    shelved with the bric-a-brac,
    downtown New Haven thrust up, ankle-high,
    its enterprise above the steel-trussed stone
    of blueprint-gothic Yale, whose spires too soon
    had splintered below the reach of virgin sky.
Leaving long cool drinks on a shady porch,
    we stunned our eyes with sun drinking the bay
    quicksilvered brim to brim immense and bent
    (there once upon a time a Pilgrim boy
    had seen ghost-sails) and walked where stunted plants
    undid their leaves to scorch
    and one lone pine, sparse feathers, bony skin,
    endured the niggard rock and naked weather,
    lashing itself from adamant to ether
    a starved wing by a monster claw outgrown.

So why'd we come? I think it had been you
   suggested casually we take the climb,
   and we had hardly stopped our conversation,
   got up, and gone; but part of me ran some-
   where up ahead to ferret out a vision,
   wishing the farther view
   might raise a glittering grail to startled hands
   or a bush burn. Maybe it was the drink
   and walking in the sun that made me think
   life could be taken where our tenure ends.
"Pure light and farness, flood and fuse the pieces
   littered about us to a perfect mirror
   and give us back our severing image clearly."
   Radio towers needled in the air;
   a bird shrieked once and then kept silence. "Surely
   here all pursuit ceases":
   for we had reached the country's very term.
   You leaned against a crevice blazed with sun
   and smiled at me, the hard light baffled on
   the sweat-flecked khaki of your uniform.
Due east lay Europe, Asia dark beyond,
   and the breeze gently playing with your hair
   was in that east bomb-blasted yesterday
   perhaps, but reaching us so faintly there
   from having crossed the void neutrality.
   Then into it I turned,
   into the vague ring of water and sky:
   "Let nothing hold; all plunges down and shatters
   for no good reason; nothing really matters,"
   leaning out to the sun like a blind eye.
That was the only further sight to see,
   our steep road having ended on bare rock.

116

till I could see again in turning back
my shadow wavering on the worn ground
and you looking at me.
We said nothing. Both of us started down
together just as though there'd been a sign,
down past the painted warnings and the pine.
As we went down, our backs were to the sun.
The sun at our backs colored all the land.
We went down watching buildings, trees, and cars
slowly grow larger than ourselves until
they took us in. When we looked up, of course
East Rock was just a high, bare, rusty hill
plumed with a pine-spray and
no more the claw-clutched verge of all we knew.
"In distance, revelation": which was all,
for we were hungry, dazed with alcohol
and the hot sunlight. We had had the view.

FOUND IN A BOTTLE

Before the ship went down, we dreamed an island Eden:
 where bland surf nestled gently on some warm, white sands,
 fawn-skinned girls would offer fruits from little hands.
 The violent mine brought quick release to seek that garden.
Our complicated cruiser buckled like a hulk
 possessed, listed, and sank–and with it, our whole onus,
 leaving to us desire, our fate free as the pinnace
 whose tiller we were holding for our own good luck.
And all seemed possible and plain; the sea lay calm
 and open to the islands through our ensign's skill.
 We rowed singing. But in the dark what snarl of will
 swerved us round to flotsam at dawn, a boatswain's sundered arm?
The ensign got it, but we must have guessed our hearts
 are circular. We held her southeast. And the thirst
 was on us. Some still doggedly sang–they were the worst.
 All night our sleep was walking streets of swarming ports.
All day the breathless sunblaze dazed the air, no sail
 could swell, the flat sea flashed up blind as lapsed illusion.
 On minimum rations we still had a week's provision
 of hardtack, but less water. Now the days waste all.
At night cold stars amaze the deeps, our earlier dream
 returns, lecherous hags squatting on fresh wells.
 We caught three flying fish. No rain yet. Nothing else–
 the sea, the sky, and where they meet, the seamless rim.
I write this with my excrement to caulk it away
 in a dry bottle, hoping that will keep it dry;
 at the mote in the midst of the blank eye of sea and sky
 I throw it to the providence of the sky and sea.

118   NOCTURNE

The page is from Life: smouldering human meat,
    a warehouse full, corrupts the air; the burgher
    S S man and jack-booted girl still must
    jerk at the foulness. Our soldiers gave the order.
Not that their game spoils me for happiness:
    I'll sleep later—would virtue suffer least?
    only, those steaming corpses aren't quite nice,
    that's all, and leave a gnawing hour to lust.
I haven't been to war; I wasn't fit:
    that harries me more in my insomnia—
    Christ, to have missed it! Then, that much enforced,
    mind shrinks to its piecework for the next day
the same as those sickened scavengers who haul
    the world with the world's waste into a hole.

AUBADE

O future, dawn and wake us tossers who
    mumble a great tongue slicker-slack and screw
    our lids down tight for stewing over you,
O future, dawn, for you are all our prayer
    and fear, and what is worse and better there
    is here our wet rose dream, our gray nightmare:
O future dawn, streak long sunlight on
    this wasting sandstone, crack the regal yawn!
    Your lovers stridulate: Oblivion!
O Future! Dawn!

POPULAR SONG

Come, dear, let's lie together
    and mingle one another,
    chip off a chunk before we're on the shelf.
    Of course the doing's hackneyed,
    you're pimpled and I'm knock-kneed;
    but central keeps on asking, Number please?
Kissing till early morning
    won't likely end our yearning:
    just see the swarming herds that haunt my sneeze!
    and rounder than an apple,
    firmer than any nipple,
    I love myself, my dear, I love myself.
If I say, Never leave me
    or some such, please forgive me
    confusing flight with falling in the gulf.
    War creates nice diversions,
    all corners sell abortions,
    and central keeps on asking, Number please?
Right now we like each other
    perhaps, but it seems rather
    boring to hang around in the same old squeeze.
    H-bombs are quite exciting,
    and I need stimulating
    to love myself, my dear, to love myself.

Amy Clampitt '41   121

In the entire history of late-bloomers, there must be
precious few to equal Amy Clampitt. The critical
celebration of her first book-length collection of poems
would have seemed remarkable under any circum-
stances. But Amy was over 60 when *The Kingfisher* was
published in 1983. Moreover, these poems cut sharply
against the grain of contemporary taste. Her poems had
begun to appear in *The New Yorker* in 1978, but even so
The Kingfisher was not what anyone was expecting.
This debut, as brilliant as it was belated, was followed
by 10 years of remarkable productivity that yielded four
more volumes of poetry, each of which added to her
stature and brought her a place among American poets
that very few could challenge.

Amy Clampitt was born and raised in the Quaker
community of New Providence, Iowa. After graduating
from Grinnell, she went to New York City and spent
most of the remainder of her life there, doing editorial
work, participating in the civil rights and peace
movements of the '60s, and working for the Audubon
Society. Some time after the publication of a small
volume of poems (*Multitudes, Multitudes*) in 1974, her
work began to appear regularly in journals and maga-
zines. The titles of her full-length collections are *The
Kingfisher* (1983), *What the Light Was Like* (1985),
Archaic Figure (1987), *Westward* (1990), and *A Silence
Opens* (1993). All her poetry was brought together in
The Collected Poems of Amy Clampitt, with a foreword

122   by Mary Jo Salter (1997). There is also a collection of
her literary essays, *Predecessors, Et Cetera* (1991).

Among the many distinctions bestowed upon Amy
Clampitt was a Guggenheim Fellowship, an honorary
doctorate from Grinnell College, and an award in
literature from the American Academy and Institute of
Arts and Letters. She was a writer in residence at several
colleges and universities and in 1992 was made a
MacArthur Prize Fellow.

Culture and nature were equally exciting to Amy
Clampitt—as were both past and present, both words
and things, both long views and amazing close-ups.
("Excited" is a hard word to avoid in connection with
both her personality and her poems.) To say that she
was inordinately bookish in no sense denies her
constant alertness to the world beyond the printed
page; she wholeheartedly endorsed the judgment of
Wallace Stevens—a judgment reflected in all her
poetry—that the worst poverty is not to live in a
physical world. Making one's way through a Clampitt
poem can be a daunting challenge, owing mainly, I
would say, to the way her thought often leaps—within
her astounding range of reference—from one area of
experience to another, from the immediacy of a
particular locale, for instance, to her reading, or to
personal recollections, or even to a public issue or
yesterday's news. When successful, this produces not
mere flightiness but a rich layering that in the end
suggests, rather than fragmentation and dispersal, a
wholeness of view and a deep core of quietness—or
even quietism—beneath the stir and hubbub.

Has any other American writer taken more thoroughly to heart those authors we think of as the mainstays of an "English literature survey"? I have included one of her several poems about British authors, which represent an important side of her work, but such poems assume detailed familiarity with literary biography. "Highgate Cemetery" has largely to do with George Eliot's bravely unconventional personal life, her liaison with G.H. Lewes, and especially her eventual marriage to John Cross, a man much younger than herself. Amy Clampitt's faithfulness to canonized British writers and her fondness for their home ground has led one critic to complain of her "rather overawed anglophilia." It is something that began at least as far back as her high school literature class and grew as she became increasingly familiar with England itself. Her first visit there, she claimed, "changed my life forever"; and Oxford was "where for the first time I believed that the past could be experienced as something present."

England's past and its literature weren't by any means her only source of inspiration. There was Greece, Italy, the ever-fascinating Manhattan, and many other parts of America. Not least of these was her native Iowa. But even there, and certainly everywhere else, her typical relation to the scene was that of "an intensely interested visitor" who felt "nowhere wholly at home." She was therefore particularly fortunate to have, in Harold Korn, a friend of long standing to support her sense of stability and confidence. They married in 1994, the last year of Amy's life, and bought a home in Lenox, Mass.

BEACH GLASS

While you walk the water's edge,
turning over concepts
I can't envision, the honking buoy
serves notice that at any time
the wind may change,
the reef-bell clatters
its treble monotone, deaf as Cassandra
to any note but warning. The ocean,
cumbered by no business more urgent
than keeping open old accounts
that never balanced,
goes on shuffling its millenniums
of quartz, granite and basalt.

                          It behaves
toward the permutations of novelty–
driftwood and shipwreck, last night's
beer cans, split oil, the coughed-up
residue of plastic–with random
impartiality, playing catch or tag
or touch-last like a terrier,
turning the same thing over and over,
over and over. For the ocean, nothing
is beneath consideration.

                        The houses
of so many mussels and periwinkles
have been abandoned here, it's hopeless
to know which to salvage. Instead
I keep a lookout for beach glass–
amber of Budweiser, chrysoprase

of Almadén and Gallo, lapis
by way of (no getting around it,
I'm afraid) Phillips'
Milk of Magnesia, with now and then a rare
translucent turquoise or blurred amethyst
of no known origin.
                The process
goes on forever: they came from sand,
they go back to gravel,
along with the treasuries
of Murano, the buttressed
astonishments of Chartres,
which even now are readying
for being turned over and over as gravely
and gradually as an intellect
engaged in the hazardous
redefinition of structures
no one has yet looked at.

THE WOODLOT

Clumped murmuring above a sump of loam–
grass-rich, wood-poor–that first the plow,
then the inventor (his name plowed under
somewhere in the Patent Office) of barbed wire,
taught, if not fine manners, how at least to follow
the surveyor's rule, the woodlot nodes of willow,
evergreen or silver maple gave the prairie grid
what little personality it had.
                              Who could
have learned fine manners where the air,
that rude nomad, still domineered,
without a shape it chose to keep,
oblivious of section lines, in winter
whisking its wolfish spittle to a froth
that turned whole townships into
one white wallow? Barbed wire
kept in the cattle but would not abrade
the hide or draw the blood
of gales hurled gnashing like seawater over fences'
laddered apertures, rigging the landscape
with the perspective of a shipwreck. Land-chained,
the blizzard paused to caterwaul
at every windbreak, a rage the worse
because it was in no way personal.
                              Against
the involuted tantrums of spring and summer–
sackfuls of ire, the frightful udder

of the dropped mammocumulus
become all mouth, a lamprey
swigging up whole farmsteads, suction
dislodging treetrunks like a rotten tooth–
luck and a cellarhole were all
a prairie dweller had to count on.
         Whether
the inventor of barbed wire was lucky
finally in what he found himself
remembering, who knows? Did he
ever, even once, envision
the spread of what he'd done
across a continent: whale-song's
taut dulcimer still thrumming as it strung together
orchard, barnyard, bullpen, feedlot,
windbreak: wire to be clambered over,
crawled through or slid under, shepherded–
the heifers staring–to an enclosure
whose ceiling's silver-maple tops
stir overhead, uneasy, in the interminably
murmuring air? Deep in it, under
appletrees like figures in a ritual, violets
are thick, a blue cellarhole
of pure astonishment.
         It is
the earliest memory. Before it,
I/you, whatever that conundrum may yet
prove to be, amounts to nothing.

128   GOOSEBERRY FOOL

The gooseberry's no doubt an oddity,
an outlaw or pariah even–thorny
and tart as any
kindergarten martinet, it can harbor
like a fernseed, on its leaves' under-
side, bad news for pine trees,
whereas the spruce
resists the blister rust
it's host to. That veiny Chinese
lantern, its stolid jelly
of a fruit, not only has
no aroma but is twice as tedious
as the wild strawberry's sunburst
stem-end appendage: each one must
be between-nail-snipped at both extremities.

Altogether, gooseberry virtues
take some getting
used to, much as does trepang,
tripe à la mode de Caen,
or having turned thirteen.
The acerbity of all things green
and adolescent lingers in
it–the arrogant, shrinking,
prickling-in-every-direction thorn-
iness that loves no company except its,
or anyhow that's what it gets:
bristling up through gooseberry ghetto sprawl
are braced thistles' silvery, militantly symmetrical

defense machineries. Likewise inseparably en-
tangled in the disarray of an
uncultivated childhood, where gooseberry bushes (since
rooted out) once flourished, is
the squandered volupté of lemon-
yellow-petaled roses' luscious flimflam—
an inkling of the mingling into one experience
of suave and sharp, whose supremely im-
probable and far-fetched culinary
embodiment is a gooseberry fool.

Tomorrow, having stumbled into
this trove of chief ingredients
(the other being very thickest cream)
I'll demonstrate it for you. Ever since,
four summers ago, I brought you,
a gleeful Ariel, the trophy
of a small sour handful,
I've wondered what not quite articulated thing
could render magical
the green globe of an unripe berry.
I think now it was simply
the great globe itself's too much to carry.

130 HIGH CULTURE

The geranium and the begonia
bloom with such offhand redundance
we scarcely notice. But the
amaryllis is a study in

disruption: everything routine
gives way to the unsheathing
of its climbing telescope—
a supernova of twin crimson

tunnels, porches of infinity
where last week there was nothing.
Months of clandestine preparation
now implode in pollen

that will never brush a bee,
fueling the double-barreled velvet
stairwell of its sterile pistils
with a tapered incandescence

that's already short of breath
and going blind before a
week is out. Such show
of breeding, such an excess

of cultivation, all but asks us
to stop breathing too until
it's over. I remember
how, the night the somewhat

famous violinist came to supper,
the whisper of the gown she
put on just before the concert
filled the parlor of the farmhouse

with things it had no room for—
the slave marts of the East,
the modes of Paris, the gazing
ramparts of the stratosphere.

HIGHGATE CEMETERY

Laid in unconsecrated ground, a scandal
still–note how good Gerard Hopkins
recoiled from what a queer, awkward girl,
frail-shouldered, massive, rickety,
volcanic, out of an unconsecrated
attachment, a marriage that was
no marriage (one would have added,
till opprobrium intervened, *but
something better*) to a pockmarked
lightweight of a drama critic,
saw blossom: this domestic improbability,
this moonflower: they were happy.

Happiness: *that*–as it always has been–
was the scandal. As for the uninhibited
pursuit of same, gone merrily
amok, by now, among the lit-up
purlieus of a game show (died
of a conniption, beaming): time
spared her that, though not the cold shoulder,
the raw east wind, fog, the roar that issues
from the other side of silence; not headache,
kidney stone, the ravages of cancer–or
of grief foreseen, met with, engulfed by,
just barely lived through.

Nature (she'd written, years before) *repairs
her ravages, but not all. The hills
underneath their green vestures bear*

the marks of past rending. Johnny Cross,   **133**
younger by two decades, a banker,
athletic, handsome, read Dante with her,
fell in love; repeatedly, distressingly,
spoke of marriage, was at last accepted.
Another scandal–in the eyes of devotees
who looked on marrying at all with horror
as for the breathing fishbowl of appearances.
Grotesque, my dear. An episode in Venice,
on their honeymoon (who knows what makes any
of us do what we do?) was somehow weathered.
Then, in six months, she was dead.

At Highgate, the day she was buried,
a cold rain fell, mixed with snow. Slush
underfoot. Mud tracked inside the chapel.
Her brother Isaac, more than twenty years estranged
(a ravage never healed), was there
among the mourners–hordes of them,
the weather notwithstanding. Edith Simcox,
crazed with devotion to this woman who'd been,
in her ill-favored way, so beautiful, arrived
with a nosegay of violets, wandered off distracted
into the dusk, came to herself finally
at a station she didn't recognize,
somewhere in Hampstead.

In rain-wet May, not quite a century later–
cow parsley head-high, the unkempt
walks a blur, faint drip of birdsong,
ivy taking over–the stone is hard to find.

134

Herbert Spencer, a creature of exemplary
good sense, however ill-equipped
for rapture, lies buried not far off,
his monumental neighbor a likeness
of Karl Marx, egregious in granite—
godfather of such looked-for victories
over incorrigible Nature, his memory red
with nosegays ribboned in Chinese.

A WINTER BURIAL

From tall rooms, largesse of peonies,
the porches summercool, the bed upstairs
immaculate in its white counterpane,

to kerosene-lit evenings, the wind
an orphan roaming the silver maples,
sudden widowhood: to meaner comforts,

a trumpetvine above the kitchen door,
then one night her new husband didn't
come in from the milking: to the lot

she bought with what that place went
for, dwindlings in a doll's house: to
the high-rise efficiency condominium,

television on all day, to the cubicle
in the denominational home, to total
unprivacy of bed and bedpan, nurse shoes,

TV with no picture or else coming in waves,
a vertigo: to, one nightfall when the last
weak string gave way that had held whatever

she was, that mystery, together, the bier
that waited–there were no planes coming in,
not many made it to the funeral, the blizzard

136

had been so bad, the graveyard drifted
so deep, so many severed limbs of trees
thrown down, they couldn't get in to plow

an opening for the hearse, or shovel
the cold white counterpane from that cell
in the hibernal cupboard, till the day after.

PAUMANOK

The humped, half-subterranean
    potato barns, the tubers
like grown stones, wet meat
    from underground a bused-in,
moved-on proletariat once
    stooped for, where Paumanok's
outwash plain, debris of glaciers,
    frays to a fishtail,

now give place to grapevines,
    their tendency to ramble
and run on, to run to foliage
    curbed, pruned, trained
into another monoculture—row
    after profitable row
on acre after acre, whole landscapes
    strung like a zither

where juniper and honeysuckle,
    bayberry, Virginia creeper,
goldenrod and poison ivy would
    have rioted, the wetlands
glistening at the margin, the reed-
    bed plumes, the groundsel's
tideline windrows a patina of
    perpetual motion

138

washed by the prevailing airs,
   where driven human
diligence alone could, now or ever,
   undo the uninstructed
thicketing of what keeps happening
   for no human reason,
one comes upon this leeward, mowed
   and tended pocket,

last resting place of slaves, each
   grave marked by a boulder
hardly more than a potato's size,
   unnamed but as dependents of
Seth Tuthill and his wife Maria,
   who chose finally to lie here
   with their sometime chattels,
   and whose memory too is now
   worn down to stone.

Mary A. Pryor '47   **139**

A native of Massachusetts but a long-time resident of
Moorhead, Minn., where until her retirement in 1992
she was professor of English at Moorhead State
University, Mary A. Pryor has studied nursing at Yale
University School of Nursing (M.N.), drama at the Yale
School of Drama, and English literature at the Univer-
sity of Nebraska (M.A., Ph.D.).

As Mary Pryor puts it, "I write verse steadily."
Among the many publications in which her work has
appeared are *Poetry Digest, American Poets and Poetry,
North Coast Review, Red Weather, Plains Poetry Journal,
Plainswoman, The Tenth Muse,* and *Six Poets of the Red
River.* Two of her collections of poetry have been
published by the Territorial Press, Moorhead State
University. She has given poetry readings on public
radio, at her university, and in art galleries and similar
venues, including "the gazebo in Island Park."

This selection suggests something of Mary Pryor's
range (from painters to poets, from butterflies to
waterbeds) and her alert and resourceful poetic impulse.

GEORGIA O'KEEFFE AT EIGHTY-FOUR

With rocks and bones and brushes in the sun,
adobe walls so weathered and refined
the blood and ocher mesas of the mind
go gamboling and ghostly rivers run
broad in their flood-gouged channels, as begun
the work proceeds, the fiery blue outlined
by bony socket, onyx veins entwined
in rock. The colors radiate and stun.
Between the concept and the canvas, gone
all barrier, so sure the hand, unswerving.
Wakes on a roof...the chrysolite of dawn...
owns dogs and turkeys...little use for words...
lives painting, planting, pruning and preserving,
and playing Monteverdi to her birds.

MONARCHS

With apology to
Magic Realists and Environmentalists

I took it for a myth that butterflies
travel in clouds, in droves,
that women can be gowned before our eyes
naked as cloves
yet virtually modest, that in shrouds
of butterflies, in state,
the greatest heroes lie, while weeping crowds
file by. Those who migrate
require strength. What fancy of demented
or visionary brain
supposed that hordes of butterflies frequented
the hallowed high terrain
of mountain pine groves, annually, soared
reclaiming their august
domain until assembled wing-beats roared?
Alas—vermilion dust!
It was the truth. It cannot be restored.

MIGRATION

To find my yard, this casual residence
a node, a station in a cosmic grid
shivers the senses, blows the lid
on patterns, powers, evidence
that negligence or mere distraction hid.

By force fields, guts of time, tuned pole to pole,
voyagers bent on water, black oil seed,
find caravansaries that feed
quick-blooded wings that shuttle goal
to goal, from southern pleasures, home to breed.

The winter residents: house finch, woodpecker;
the summer robin, mourning dove, and wren;
defer to transients–"Thrush again."
"Rose breasted grosbeak!" Bird Baedecker
marks urban yard and tags calcareous fen.

Mapped on the tender parchment of the brain,
knitted by instinct in a global net,
the bobolink and avocet,
the humming bird and swan, contain
trails known to those that have not flown them yet.

BALLADE FOR EMILY DICKINSON

For me, she walks in damask and in furs,
barefooted, regal, on the ledge-hewn side
of thunder clouds where purple lightning stirs.
Forget the "Belle of Amherst," one who shied
from guests, baked ginger cake, steeped tea, till dried
up spinster-wise at last to sit alone
upstairs in white, a wilted jilted, bride,
for Dickinson knew "Zero at the Bone."

Even her whimsicality avers
stark undertones. That clover prairie-wide,
that robin rowing air, plant cosmic burs
to instigate our dreams. How she could chide
unearthly powers as equals! Deified
and damned, she spoke defiance, not a moan,
and scorned submission, in unblemished pride,
for Dickinson knew "Zero at the Bone."

On scaffolds of the mind, one slip incurs
the plunge into an existential tide,
yet here she balances. The game is hers
in matters of the soul. She needs no guide
to probe eternity and dares confide
in immortality–enshrined, unknown.
A carriage drive? No, a Valkyrie ride,
for Dickinson knew "Zero at the Bone."

She heard a Fly buzz, heard the stars collide
and heard the mosses creeping up a stone,
explored the brim where death and life divide,
for Dickinson knew "Zero at the Bone."

144   IF RAIN

> If you had never seen it rain, how you would marvel
> at the dull aluminum scrim, the landscape striated
> vertically or aslant, stretched on the bias,
> at how surfaces pock or erupt into gooseflesh
> and how the bird bath sprouts momentary mushrooms,
> everything latticed or glazed, just shy of gleaming
> under the muted storm light.
>
> Think, if you came from a region where water was cherished
> in jugs and bags and bottles, even a brackish wallow
> pitted with hoof and paw prints celebrated in song
> as an oasis. Think of wringing your own sweat
> out of a shirt to moisten a mouth full of ashes.
> Think of the ultimate hospitality of washing the feet of a guest.
>
> Then watch the rain. Does the grass bend under duress
> or shiver and flex in homage, perceptibly greening?

REFUSAL TO BUY A WATERBED

It's not so much the dread of sagging joists
nor thrift that calculates the cost of current
nor that propensity to *mal de mer*
(legacy of a carsick child)
nor thought of rousing
on nights of blizzard to a power outage
and clammy linen.
It's not even–although it crossed my mind–electrocution.

Nor is it the young couple, years ago,
in the basement apartment,
their storms, typhoons, and shipwrecks,
the leaks they sprang, flooding the laundry room
and nearly asphyxiating themselves by trying to mend
punctures with tire patch and lethal solvent.

No. In the main, I shudder
at prospect, one thin skin away, one membrane
from the tip of my vulnerable nose,
of a virtual ocean,
of gulfs and straits and archipelagos
and measureless Bermuda triangles
where lodestones go berserk
and molds and mildews, microbes, many-tentacled
hydras, and jelly-fish, Charybdis, Scylla,
and lantern-jawed illuminated monsters
hunt, kill, eat, breed in anaerobic darkness.

Hearken! They slosh within
an eyelash of our dreams.

146   *Mary D. Parsons Burkett '48*

Mary Parsons Burkett, a native of Eagle Grove, Iowa, now living in Paw Paw, Mich., recalls an interest in poetry from her earliest years, being enthralled by Stevenson's *A Child's Garden of Verses* and A. A. Milne's *When We Were Six* well before Mary herself was 6, and writing her first poem at age 7. While majoring in music at Grinnell College, Mary Parsons trained as a lyric soprano and choral specialist, experience that has sustained a lifelong involvement in teaching and performing music. She notes that her study and performance of both art songs and choral works, whose nuances of text deserve careful attention, contribute to a happy symbiosis between her professional activities in music and her avocation as a writer of verse.

As an undergraduate Mary Parsons published poems in *The Tanager*, Grinnell's literary magazine that reached well beyond the campus for its contributors (an interesting assortment that includes Carl Sandburg, Eudora Welty, Jessamyn West, Louis L'Amour, Paul Engle, and Pablo Neruda) before it ceased operations in 1948, the year she graduated. Her poetry has appeared in *A Black River Syllabary*, a literary magazine originating in South Haven, Mich.; and some of her work was chosen for "poetry on the bus" in a competition held by the Kalamazoo Metro Transit System.

Gentle, lyrical, often wistful—Mary Parsons Burkett's poems can show a hard edge as satisfying as the calm, resonant music that echoes through them.

A PROMISE BROKEN   147

I said I would not weep,
But things there are
That only tears can free:
Old griefs that dry
Within the heart still pent
Turn into bitterness, and I
Would rather play the fool an hour
Than give my life to sorrow;
So I cry my anguish to the winds,
And do not borrow from the future's joy.
I think he would not mind this giving way,
For he too knew
That tears are for today,
But silence is a long time being spent.

148   UNREQUITED

There is a rim around this sky–
Somewhere, beyond it, on another curve of earth
The boy I love draws breath, and laughs and dreams,
A perfect entity,
In spite of being thus removed from me.
Perhaps it's just as well he does not know
My life is half itself without him here.
That I should love him, agony enough;
That he should know it, more than I could bear!

POST WAR PLAN   149

I'll go to a field where daisies blow
And grass grows deep and warm with sun;
Where time is lazy-like and slow,
And golden hours like honey run
Across my consciousness to fill
With separate tiny drops my cup
Of living to the brim, until
It surfeits me to drink it up.

I will make a daisy chain,
Each flower a glowing, separate joy,
Each for a memory, bright with pain,
And a pledge I made to a lonely boy.
There on his hill I'll fashion flowers
Blessed by the sky and summer's breath,
In the name of his yesterday's happy hours,
And today's perfect circle of life and death.

MOON LIB

The tree clasps the moon in boney arms,
Caressing her fullness with frozen fingers.
"Ah! You are mine…You belong to me!"

"Your prisoner, sire," discrete, she sighs,
But as the minutes glide
She coolly slips away, although the tree,
And many trees, stretch tiptoe after her.

ON SNOWSHOES   **151**

The month it snowed and snowed, we strode,
Mammoth-footed, across the battened lake
Whose feet were usually moated by the springtime rains,
Defended by a thousand stinging hosts in summertime,
So they had seemed remote as Xanadu.
Seeking the deer, who had a prior claim,
We found them banished by the white terrain
That gave us access to their private sanctuary.
Leaving our fanshaped tracks for squirrels to wonder at,
We reached a whitened twenty acre page
Where rabbit feet had scrawled a message:
"Hunger!" but had not despaired.
The cornstalks marked out treasure trove;
Like pirate digs, the tunnels led to buried gold
On Mother Earth's dark breast.
The south wind stung our faces,
Burrowed into pockets, but the sun
Reflected from a billion tiny mirrors,
Warmed our backs. Deliberate as ducks,
Eastward we walked, on water and on air,
Over the great, smooth wind-sculpt haunch of winter
And the slumbering raspberry patch,
Toward home.

AUGUST MORNING

Only the mourning doves call now;
Mating's outrageous flirting
And the nest bound chatter of the hungry young
Are silenced.

The wind sings in the leaves
The dryer song of coming fall.
It speaks my season,
The slow and silent ache of aging.

The accusations of the katydids
Are ceaselessly reciting all my sins:
"She did!" "She didn't!"
Above the litany of cricket sounds.

Curtis Harnack '49   **153**

Though known particularly as a prose writer (admired by the likes of John Gardner and Raymond Carver), Curtis Harnack has also published poetry in a wide variety of literary magazines, including *American Poetry Review, Sewanee Review, The Nation, Salmagundi, The New Criterion, The Ontario Review*, and *Southwest Review*.

Curt, as he was always known at Grinnell, grew up in rural western Iowa but received some of his education and has lived most of his professional life "back East," especially in New York City. His work reflects an attachment to both environments. After serving in the U.S. Navy during World War II, Curt graduated from Grinnell in 1949, won a Lydia Roberts Fellowship to Columbia University, and earned an M.A. in literature. Then it was back to Iowa to teach at Grinnell and in the University of Iowa Writer's Workshop and to work with Paul Engle as co-editor of two annual volumes of the prize stories in the O'Henry Memorial Collection. He later taught at Sarah Lawrence and Williams Colleges and for 16 years was the executive director of Yaddo, the retreat for artists in Saratoga Springs, N.Y. More recently he was president and CEO of the School of American Ballet, the official training school of the New York City Ballet. In 1991 he served as chairman of the fiction panel for the National Book Awards.

Curt Harnack's career as a writer may have had to

154

compete with these other varied and demanding responsibilities, but that has not prevented him from producing an impressive body of characteristically well-made, deeply felt, and quietly resonant work. He has distinguished himself in many different forms, beginning with the publication of a novel in 1960 (*The Work of an Ancient Hand*) and including three memoirs (*Persian Lions, Persian Lambs*; *We Have All Gone Away*; and *The Attic*), a history (*Gentlemen on the Prairie*), other novels (*Love and Be Silent* and *Limits of the Land*), and a collection of short fiction (*Under My Wings Everything Prospers*). His poems are an illuminating complement to these prose works.

Honored by numerous awards both for his writing and for his work in behalf of the arts, Curt received a Grinnell College Alumni Citation in 1974 and a Litt.D. degree from his alma mater in 1986.

He is married to the noted American fiction writer, Hortense Calisher.

THE NEARNESS

It takes the off-moment
when not really looking
to see the wary red fox
or the silent snowy owl
directly over one's head
when walking in the woods.

Note the ancient apple trees
pretending to be young,
a gaudy heft to their limbs;
or the sudden mushrooms
strenuously at work lifting
thatches of pine needles.

Withhold that heavy boot
from a furze of red lichen,
let the white violet be:
go deliberately looking
and you'll never find
what is best out here.

Catch them at their living,
but no one must know;
not even myself or you.

WEARING A
NOISE PROTECTOR
IN MANHATTAN

Can't stand much more of it:
two piping signals and the blast
comes next – *Whee*, it's all clear,
so I buy these wraps for ears
grown tender to sound abrasives.
Now just look at me, geared for
the extraterrestrial, perhaps in
reaches of silence too artificial
to be bearable, an alternative to
ruckus that seems overly complete.
I've taken myself into the inmost
whorl of a seashell, tightened
around the last curve of silence,
earmuffed here to all assaults
Acoustical, in a cocoon so deadened
the world has largely gone; my own
blood seems unable to reach me,
my thoughts, meant to be protected,
crowd at snaffled barriers of foam,
struggling to escape solitary.

Oh, if I could think of myself as
a crewman on an airport runway
waving signal bats, guiding 747s
into fragile berths where accordian
esophagi hook up air carriers
to their little purposes of people;

or a goggled Con Ed repairman
drilling for cables in asphalt;
a duck hunter crouching too close
to murder; maybe even a gunnery
range sergeant; or a farmer driving
a combine across wheat fields –
these handymen of the necessary,
attenuating their occupational noise
this way. But I'm just sitting here
defensively, all of you getting remote,
the clamp on my head a mechanical
sedative.

        If you call, don't expect
me to answer, you're too far away.
I hear only the dull thud of bones
hitting the floor when I walk,
plus the trickle of secretions
flowing in or out of my ears,
and the bellows of my lungs.
Should I speak (just now tried),
it comes out a universal *ummm*;
my grinding jaw and clicking teeth
are newly known to me. In this
sound room I prefer not to move
at all, awaiting the appearance
of what I have been saved from.

158   EPITHALAMIUM

I found my Mother's
pink wedding nightgown
in an attic trunk,
still faintly stained
with hymenal blood,
after that night
perhaps never worn,
and removed it
from the deserted house,
a present for my wife
who's nearly the same size.
She noticed the brown streak
—but such lovely fabric,
and put the shift on.

Yes, yes, how it falls
over breasts and hips,
shimmering rosy silk
soft as American beauty
petals, delicious to touch,
clinging to my fingers
with static like memory.
Did I imagine eros
would bloom easily
with this bridal cloth—
that we could soar high
over such a history?
here in the bed our
flesh seems tangled.

For we are caught
in a weal of time,
the silky, slippery fabric
moves between us almost
alive—telling me,
telling me otherwise.

UNION SQUARE MARKET

It's a fair, an outdoor bazaar,
my shopping bags quickly fill:
organic fruit, seven-grain bread,
distressed-looking vegetables,
so real after glossy supermarket
displays from distant California,
a heavy load to plop down before
yet another stall, appraising
the greens while a black woman
ahead of me counts out pennies,
her body thick with layerings
against the cold; brindled scraps,
feet shod in Adidas discards
from which her bunions poke,
sacks of scavengings under her,
treasure gleaned from the streets,
her hoard of coppers perhaps
plucked from the sidewalks.

You and I have seen them
glinting in asphalt, but over one
cent are too privileged to stoop;
we ignore the jars for these
nuisance pennies next to cash
registers, being far beyond
caring about such chickenfeed.

She harvested those pennies,
stacks them here like tiny tubular
skyscrapers that line Third Avenue,
making a city in model before
its conversion into food.
                    "Take
your time," says the farmwife,
remarkably tender toward her.

We two are suppliants before
earth's valid representative,
approach the laden table of
the Lord in equal standing. I
encounter this street-neighbor
not through a confrontational
"Put money in the cup!" or alms-
sympathy of the kind evoked by
the pieta outside Carnegie Hall,
holding a sign, "Dying of AIDS,"—
one's defensive numbness in
place, so that it's hard to move.

Here she is for the same reason
as you and indifferent to your
presence. You aren't anything
to her, while she exercises her
right to exist. Both of you eat to
live: you cannot turn away.

EARLY CAMERA-WORK

They're game and don't move,
innocent of the long-term
uses to be made of them

Stillness required yet none
takes the posing seriously—
hold it!—no frantic clicks

As with modern photographers
hoping one take out of twenty
catches a moment no ordinary.

Their bodies might be dummies,
so drained of life, a wrapping
of clothes without authenticity.

These droll subjects submit
themselves to pooled time,
don't just stop their lives

But arrest the onward movement
of their innermost selves,
seemingly not modern even then.

Yet their eyes find a route
through the aperture of the box
facing them, as we with space

Optics probe the cataract
of galaxies, peering into
outer reaches of the universe.

163

What they see I know
in a way they couldn't:
how anybody's current reality

Falls apart over time,
our nimble photographer
himself in some images,

The timer allowing him to be
both perpetrator and victim,
gazing out with the same emptiness.

164   BALLET STUDENTS
          IN STREET-CLOTHES

When they subscribe to
convention and wear garments
like other mortals, honoring
the nostalgia of the ordinary,
it's a relief for them. Yet
their perfected bodies are
too hidden, fashion state-
ments seems beside the point.

Girls clad in flowing shifts,
scarcely any sign of breasts,
pipestem arms, walking
in clumpy mod shoes,
splay-footed, sternums high,

boys in draggy jeans,
floppy T's, slouching along
disguised as their peers,
disappearing from public
notice, an excessiveness
of clothes that's touching,
almost laughable.

Imagine, those of you who
regard raiment as necessary,
what it feels like to have
no need to hide limbs –
the altar of celebration
isn't approached carnally,
one's self on display
innocently, with no intention
other than to exhibit male
or female physicality
in ideal human shape.

Before class, teenage
costumes are sloughed,
they emerge like chrysalides,
peeled to leotards and tights,
then move within rituals of
tendus and *battements*
undergone together at
the *barre* and on to travelling
bourrees, whirling pirouettes,
as they gain the air, leaping
into an elemental artifice.

Whereas clothes suggest
bonds to everyday, any time,
the depressingly finite we know,
their articulated gestures with
bodies fully exposed slip
us into a dream shared,
applause a final covering
perhaps – for us, not them.

Alan Goldfarb '52

A native of South Side Chicago, Alan Goldfarb majored in political science at Grinnell, played varsity football, put the shot on the track team, and won prizes in the Selden Whitcomb poetry contest. He earned a master's degree in public administration at Syracuse University and became an official in the U.S. Department of Housing and Urban Development. Well along into his career at HUD, Alan spent a year on sabbatical leave at the University of California and subsequently moved permanently with his wife and three children to Berkeley. In that yeasty environment he found himself involved in city government and served three productive terms on the Berkeley City Council.

Alan Goldfarb refers to himself as an amateur poet, but his work has appeared in *Poetry Northwest* and among the winners in the National Poetry Competition of 1995. As his poems make their quiet way between scrupulous nostalgia and fancy, there is a kind of reluctance about them that can appeal more solidly than any amount of compulsive, high-energy caterwauling.

His wife Arlene and son John are also Grinnell graduates.

THE SNOWDOME   **167**

It always snows on my birthday.
The snowflakes whirl and fall into the city,
filling the almost airless dome
of Manhattan. It's the present father bought
when I was sick, and couldn't take
the Pullman to New York with him.
Everyone knew they weren't real storms,
like those that closed the schools
and kept my mother at home.
Whenever I'd press the cold
marble to my head, it made me better,
so I'd ask mother if anyone could come over.
Oh, no, she'd say, afraid
I'd get sicker. And when I turned
the city over and over on my chest,
she wondered who would deliver
the milk to the children,
or feed the animals at the zoo.
It didn't matter, I told her,
filling the sky with snow, the schoolyards,
the deepening streets,
the zoo where the animals lie and wait.

THE HOUSE ON WALNUT

I'd wake up to the steam in the pipes
and the windows cracking with frost…
–then my mother's voice.
I already knew the cereal was getting cold
and I had to get dressed. I raced
all the way to school in a purple light.
My room was in front, just off the street,
then mother's room where she and father slept.
There was a tall chair and father's dresser;
I could barely reach the top–the old coins,
the bundled letters from Terezin
and the Red Cross, and photos
of cousins that almost looked like us.
At the end of the hall my brother's room,
which we kept empty. Father was too old
to go to war again. He went to work
in the black Buick before we were awake.
When he came home we'd listen
to the Lone Ranger before I went to sleep.
Was it really my life?

I circle the house again. Now it's gray
with a gray garage in back. In the dark
I can see the children running
from my room to mother's room,
then to my brother's room,
which is now a porch.
Even with my scarf up over my ears
I can hear the harsh scraping

of leaves in the trees, the distant
rumbling of a train. It's so cold
I want to go inside and say:
I lived here once when the house was white.
But I haven't a thing to offer them
under my coat. No wine, no cake, no wish
—only a child's wish.

170 THE GUEST ROOM

"Since the Lincolns never had house guests, this room
was devoted to the two younger boys, Tad and Willie."

Here on the stairs of the only home
you owned, I wonder where
your hand touched this railing I touch.
Was it here, where I touch it now?
Did you raise this curtain to the light,
just now, when the morning sun slants through?

On the second floor the guest room,
with the odd inscription by the door.
On the rug a dappled horse and a wagon,
Willie's rush-seated chair, Tad's day-bed,
an abacus, some marbles made of stone.

Willie died when he was twelve
and Tad eighteen,
hosts of a sort, guests of a sort,
in this Springfield house.

A TRIP TO FOUR TOWNS

1

It's 8 a.m....still time for a walk
beneath the willows and Norway maples,
past the swan boats
and three remaining swans.
One's been missing for several days
and they suspect foul play.
On Providence Street the rain begins,
so I drop into a coffee shop.
At my window seven hard hats
peering down a hole–until the blonde
in Reeboks dashes by. Who am I to say
they can't do this with our money?
Now to the John Hancock. I already hear
the gongs of Trinity Church
and see the giant bear
in front of F.A.O. Schwarz.
Suddenly in the east the clouds lift,
and a bird drops in silence from its V.

2

Sitting next to me on the subway,
your schoolbooks piled on your lap,
eyes half-filled with sleep,
was I ever as young as you?
Oh, I know, children are much older
than they seem. And those delicate arms
that ache from the weight
of your books–surely have embraced

172
all night the boy of your dreams,
the one who waits for you
one stop beyond where you wake up,
the place where your life begins
and ends.
              I, too, close my eyes,
rocking below the sea,
waking now to the sparrow in our car.
Did its wings touch my face?
At last it's out the door
at 42nd Street, then disappears
into the headlights of a train,
as if it were a man.

3
You wanted one last look
at the ocean, one last walk
in the granite sand. I said
I'd close the cottage,
leaving it as we found it:
porch cleared of pine needles,
blankets folded (they were still
filled with last night's sparks).
I packed the clothes you left
in the dryer–your still-damp jeans
and underthings. How small they seemed!
When I locked the door I heard
those crows in the Monterey pines.

4   173

The steely clouds give way to chaparral
and meadows, and a worm-like train.
I don't know what I expected–
giant department stores and beautiful ladies
shopping on horseback? I leave
my seat for one last stretch.
A woman of my age sees my own grayness.
Her eyes seem to say she understands
everything about me.
I smile but she turns her head
–to the same meadows, same oaks, same worm.
I must return to my seat as we
descend. When we touch down
in the unexpected rain, the oaks
are gone, and the reddish earth
moves past us in a rush.

WHERE OR WHEN

When you look at me now
we are astonished by what we see.
But haven't I seen your face
a thousand times in this light?
Haven't you seen me in your earliest dreams?
I try to follow your eyes as they turn
from the world: the park across the street,
the familiar trees,
the cottage you once named,
a name that once was mine.
I try to think: each day
will never again be the same,
even when I tell you the same
old jokes, the same old stories,
the ones you swear
you've never heard before.

Today at the ocean
we covered ourselves with sand
and fell asleep in the sun.
I dreamed the earth was flat
and you had disappeared at last.
The tide washed over us,
leaving what the sea leaves:
part of the future, part of the past.
When I awoke you gave me your lost hand.

THE REUNION

1
Hermetic night above L.A.
If we are moving and alive
it's because the stars go by.
One star falls into the wine
I hold up to the light.
      Is it too late to make a wish?
In my window my face looks back at me,
at my unfastened life.
      I haven't really thought about it lately…
As I curl into my sleep
a sudden pressure
sucks me from my seat.
The drunk across the aisle yells:
Flap your wings!
So I arch my back as best I can,
reaching my arms out
to my feathery hands
and my hands to the frozen sky.
      If they find me they will say
      I was depressed
      and fat,
      or I was high.
      And they will let it go at that.

176

2

Time to kill at the Denver airport.
Without my luggage I feel light-
headed and vaguely dispossessed.
By my gate a leftover copy
of *USA Today*, with its horrid map
of the weather.
Three moths at my window
are trying to get out of the airport.
  It distracts me just enough
   to think the largest one
    is really my airplane.
The smallest moth, exhausted now,
lands beside me on a woman's laptop.
She flicks it away in despair,
before it can work into the folds
of her skirt and the deep
heat of her thighs. It lies there
gasping on the floor, as if
it had flown already
through the yellow 70s of Colorado,
the brown 80s of Nebraska,
the red 90s of Iowa and southern Wisconsin.
Everyone seems relieved by this suffering.
  If I turn my good ear to the window
   I can almost hear my plane
    searching for the lights at our gate,
    almost bear the other two moths
    beating against the glass.

Leaving for Des Moines in the rain,
I remember a stormy commencement
all those years ago,
and the scratchy robes we wore
over our underwear.
But will I remember the names
of those I played with on the line?
Or those I might have loved
when winter turned to spring?
      And what if they ask: *You know*
      who I am, don't you? … And what
      if they wonder what I do?
Now I can almost see the college town
where two curved roads should cross.
But nothing's there,
unless it's *there*, in that stretch,
behind a cloud that covers half of it,
the half where I did my laps,
and walked in the corn with the Corn Queen
to the house we thought was empty…
On the track I can see
a figure so lean,
and the plane's shadow,
and the crow's shadow.

Merle Fischlowitz '53

Merle Fischlowitz has been a school counselor and administrator, and then for 15 years a practicing psychologist. A native of St. Louis, he has lived in Honolulu, Israel, and Washington, D.C. Currently he makes his home in San Diego, where he finds poetry writing a continuing preoccupation. His poems have appeared in *Limestone Circle*, *Sheila-Na-Gig*, and the *Sagarin Review*, and he hosts a monthly Evening of Poetry and open microphone readings at Borders Books in Mission Valley. In 1999 his first book of verse, *From Dirt Paths to Golden Streets: Poems of Immigrant Experience*, was published by North Oak Press (San Diego, Calif.).

Immigrant experience is by no means the only theme Dr. Fischlowitz treats in his poetry; but it provides him with a most distinctive unifying element, constituting an important part of his own family background and linking that to the ordeals and the hopes of other cultures, providing a source of mixed feelings and occasions for both celebration and regret.

SOUP

When my wife makes soup
to warm her lost child-years,
she cuts potatoes and carrots,
adds a great big bone,
brings them to a boil,
not in the heavy black-iron pot
her grandmother used
in the Hungarian village
but in the huge steel-clad one
her mother gave her thirty years ago.

She stirs in caraway seed–the flavor
of Budapest childhood winters–
adds more potatoes
(as many as a week's ration
at Bergen-Belsen),
a handful of pasta,
curved and stout as the women
whose pictures fill the photo albums
rescued from beneath the floor
of the bombed-out home.

She made enough for the two of us tonight,
for leftovers too,
so we'll never be starved for memories.

180   BAGELS

Brisket and matza balls,
roast chicken and noodle pudding
are too heavy, too old-fashioned
for us to eat in healthy,
modern, cholesterol-free
here-we-go-running-
into-the-21st-century
southern California heat.

But we store bagels in our freezer
for a daily breakfast treat,
as one line of prayer
from a forgotten liturgy.

AT MANZANAR

the Eastern California Park Service
will build a fence
where, once, barbed wire kept others in,
to keep out grazing cattle– and vandals
who think preserving Manzanar
is un-American.

In the high California desert
ghosted-cabin shadows surround
dusty memories of relocated internees–
Americans born of immigrant-Japanese parents,
uprooted, ripped from their farms,
homes, and stores of the new Promised Land–

relocated to protect themselves
from the threat of invasion
or the reality of hate.

Ghost shadows surround echoes of quiet chants.
An Ikibana-adorned altar stood here,
dignified center of a stopgap home,
where patient Americans waited
to begin their lives again.

I saw a lone guide appear, standing
by the stone foundation of a sentry house,
to show and tell the history of this place
from the time before the earlier invasion,
when his Paiute Indian ancestors
roamed here,
free.

ON THE MOUNTAIN

The body was pulled through the wire fence,
strands lifted by men in uniform.
He was laid on the gurney,
covered by coats and blankets,
and was gently carried
down the snow-topped mountain
to the waiting ambulance.
Pablo cried as he tried to help *La Migra*,
men he once had feared,
who saved his brother Jesus' life.

A springtime walk from a barren home,
with little food to eat, but much hope
to nourish them as they looked for work,
cutting grass or sweeping floors
in the City of Angels, they dared the nights,
the deserts, the surprising cold and heights,
where snow froze their plastic-wrapped feet.

Three days of walking without food,
one of saving warmth in a hospital room,
and again they were removed,
thrust out from this golden land,
where skiers on vacation
and police kindly give clothes
to lost and tattered beggars.

Pablo and Jesus did not meet
on a Damascus road
but were seeking their own Jerusalem.

PENNSYLVANIA AVENUE, WASHINGTON, D.C.

The fourth-generation shoe-store owner
is proud to be part of the redevelopment
of Pennsylvania Avenue,
modern, sleek, monumental.

He welcomes competition
as he sees marchers,
in protests or inaugural parades,
in this, the richest nation,
always wear shoes.

Dx: DEMENTIA, ALZHEIMER'S TYPE

Not because you bore and suckled me,
or that your patience was so often tried
by my unsuspected needs. I've cried
these silent tears and mourn the loss to me
of you, as teacher, writer, language lover,
who taught me to speak, evoke hidden thought,
find depths beyond the words, so deftly taught,
describing scene or mood, and so uncover
new truth. But now I mourn, dear Ruth, the loss
to me of your once bright cognizance;
the lonely emptiness of your mere glance,
as once supple synapses turn to dross.
Your gifts to me will never be outworn.
That you cannot know it: for this I mourn.

Robert Vas Dias '53   185

Although interested in writing from a very early age, it
was not until he came to Grinnell that Robert Vas Dias
began writing poetry ("because I thought I could,
which implies that there must have been *something*
there which encouraged me in this belief"). Poetry—his
own and also that of others—has been a large part of
his life ever since.

Vas Dias, from a family background partly
Portuguese, partly Dutch, was born in London and
grew up in New York City. After college—where he
worked on the newly established student literary
magazine, *Arena*—he served in the U.S. Army, did
editorial work for various publishers, and attended
Columbia University. During the '60s Vas Dias
founded and directed the Aspen Writers' Workshop,
conducted two poetry reading series in New York, and
established the biannual National Poetry Festival at
Michigan's Thomas Jefferson College. All the while his
own poetry was appearing widely in literary journals
and magazines, and in 1972 Bobbs-Merrill published a
major collection of his verse titled *Speech Acts and
Happenings*. He also edited the anthology *Inside Outer
Space: New Poems of the Space Age* (Doubleday-Anchor,
1970), a unique and timely acknowledgment of the first
moon landing.

In 1974 Vas Dias moved back to London where he
has played an active part in the British literary scene,
co-editing two journals (*The Atlantic Review* and *Ninth*

186   *Decade*—later *Tenth Decade*), founding Permanent Press
        as an outlet for new verse, and serving as director of the
        National Poetry Centre and general secretary of the
        Poetry Society in London. He is winner of various
        poetry fellowships and other awards and has read his
        work on radio and television, at colleges and universi-
        ties, conferences, festivals, churches, and pubs in this
        country and in the U.K. His latest book of poems is
        Time Exposures (London, Oasis, 1999).

        Among his most telling early encounters with
        serious poetry, Robert tells me, were the classroom
        study of Eliot's *The Waste Land* and a reading by
        Langston Hughes at a high school assembly. These
        posed "two conflicting ideas of poetry"—the arcane and
        the accessible—which court the skills of a subtle reader
        on the one hand and the sympathies of a careful
        observer on the other. But his own poetry, certainly full
        of subtlety and close observation, owes rather more—as
        he points out—to the example of William Carlos
        Williams than to either Hughes or Eliot.

BUDDLEIA   187

Drops in where it's not wanted
in waste ground and town garden,
cracks in the brickwork;
prises fingerlings
through basement gratings,
hangs out on worn steps
huddles, dusty in doorways
and at the base of railings, slumps
under bridges and by the roadside.

Finding what nourishment
it may even in times of drought,
it has a rickety lushness, the old soak,
and passing pedestrians pretend
to ignore its soft touch
that only butterflies return in kind.

188   WINTER: THE TWO OF US

Went walking, pavement
ringing through boot-
sole, to park
meadow, grass crackling,
ground frost-hardened—
and on the way home
a sparrow battering
a window as though no glass
divided the quick
from the slower dying.

APOTHEOSIS OF THE LINE:
AT THE STANLEY-SPENCER STUDIO SALE

As can be seen from my descriptions of this composition
[Hampstead Heath Litter, *or* The Apotheosis of Hilda]
and indeed from the way I speak about my pictures, the
chief source of feeling in composing them is what *is*
happening in them...?

—Stanley Spencer, letter to Hilda, 1954

Take a line, bend it, extend it,
circumscribe an idea for herding cattle, the line
flows from an arm extended
into the neck of a cow, *what*
is happening, the cow's haunch
becomes the man's arm
on the cow's flank, and the rest of the herd
follows from this:
Cows Being Herded.
Lines enclose cattle shapes
and the man standing, his arms
a guidepost, shouts the lines
and they heave and mass and turn
left at the edge and scuff and stamp
out of the picture.

190
Take this line into bed,
pa and ma's bed,
at the time of being a child a great
moment to me, when possibly
because I had not been well
I was in the centre of the bed,
and they were brought their breakfast;
and made the line imagine the
big black tin decorated tray
with the circles made by the cups and saucers
and the teapot and lid on the circular tray,
and at the foot of the bed the four hillocks
formed by the four sets of toes.
But where is the child, what is happening
in this scene of connubial bliss?–
ma embracing pa, the tea things
a happening on the landscape of the bed:
Mentally I have been 'bedridden' all my life.
The child is not on the bed.
Stanley's portable easel was a pram.

Make this line move, cross, connect
and reconnect; it is an idea
for figures walking, for a Resurrection,
a Visitation or *Hampstead Heath Litter*
or *The Apotheosis of Hilda.*
You are everywhere in the line,
you are in the litter which all the figures
are reading as love letters–the litter
is for them alone, each line
a letter telling of absent lovers.

Love litters this place never before made
of paper, scraps meant to be
read and taken up and assembled into
the Great Design of Things.

Carry this line into the kitchen
amongst the pots and pans and Elsie
washing up, ironing, and into
the hospital ward and bathroom where
Stanley and the orderlies scrub floors,
bathe the men, paint them
with iodine, polish the brass taps:
I have done nothing else but scrub
since I have been here.
I think it has done me good.
The line dissolves in the soapsuds
on the floor, becomes the
colour-beginning of the quotidian,
our lives in kitchens, bedrooms and bathrooms,
Stanley's soldiers forever
inspecting kit, making beds, sorting laundry,
performing ablutions:
these are the scraps of a life saved,
squared for transfer to a larger picture,
a part of the world & life of love,
a possible happening in heaven,
all the preliminary ideas and studies
for an interior, or landscape
of the divine ordinary.

192

THE LAST APPLE IN LEONIA

A small yellow planet trembling in the field
of a telescope focused on its ultimate and wobbly
sphere, the last apple in Leonia
dangles within a thicket of the firmament,
apex of a constellation of branches.

What we are seeing is but a glimmer
of pre-history, the light which sourced
the last apple in Leonia no longer with us.
It is like energy about to hatch:
as we blink and shift our lenses
it is pecked away and life slips out.

Not of this world, the last apple in Leonia
is an idea whose time has not yet arrived,
but somewhere in the garden universe
a yellow globe brims secretly again
awaiting the feathered astronomers.

A THEOLOGY

Clearly the Dawn of the Age of Flight is already fading
into jerky Movietone snow:
the medium makes the process
of throwing yourself into the firmament fundamentally
a bash, the biplane's doped linen skin
a fleshly substance you could poke
a hole in a cloud through.

But the black-robed bearded patriarch standing
on a stepladder, one hand resting on the fuselage—
a benediction? a balancing act? –is solid.
God meant man to fly,
his uprightness testifies, and who am I
to gainsay him? We do it all the time
in our streetclothes for purposes not necessarily
connected with religion. We spy in the sky.
Who knows who looks down on you?
This is a blessing, as our fathers knew
who gaped on the grass
at the first Immelmann turn.

THE RENOVATORS

194

Here they come again
those self-appointed miracle-workers, their eyes
glinting at the prospect of putting my house to rights:
ruin, ruin, ruin, is what they mean.

They walk on the roof as though it were water,
fragments spatter the walk,
fissures open in the ceiling,
rivulets run on the windowsill,
dark runnels on the walls.

Clever, these contractors
who smooth-talk me into believing
they can fix the roof because they know
a sound roof is the secret of a tranquil life.
I worry a lot about water working
its way into my house, dropping
onto my head, into my dreams, casting
me adrift, dry land out of sight,
trying to sleep in a narrow cabin,
economy class, someone tapping
on the ceiling in stiletto heels;
the waves slide by the porthole
of my long, close cabin,
the trecherous waters bathe
my body between the sticky sheets.

Norman Leer '58

Author of a groundbreaking study of one of modern
literature's major figures (*The Limited Hero in the Novels
of Ford Madox Ford* [Michigan State University Press]),
Norman Leer is professor emeritus at Roosevelt
University, where he has taught since 1967. In addition
to scholarly articles and poems appearing in several
journals, he has published three books of poetry, *I
Dream My Father in a Song*, *Slightly Crumpled Survival
Flower*, and *Second Lining* (all of them illustrated by his
wife, the Danish-born artist Grethe Brix-J. Leer). He
has been a Fulbright lecturer in English at Odense
University in Denmark, and in 1990 he was awarded
the Illinois Significant Poet's Award by state Poet
Laureate Gwendolyn Brooks.

Surely one of the most absorbing features of
Norman Leer's poetry is its varied responsiveness to the
world of music. This interest embraces both classical
music and jazz; it results in poems inspired by perform-
ers and composers, by single works and by musicians'
life experiences. As well as providing the ostensible
subject of many of Norman's poems, music—as the
object of his thoughtful listening—is the impetus for
poems that reach well beyond strictly musical preoccu-
pations.

REMEMBERING ART HODES
AT THE MAYFAIR REGENT

It was a fragile year and holy
place; calm arched windows
made a sanctuary out of palms
and silk; outside, dots
of beaded trees against the prehistoric
lake turned darkness into Christmas
light, and we went once a month,
ordered drinks and prayed.

He and the piano sat; its legs
were his, his hands the keys,
hunched in excavation. His head
danced and brooded, inventing
commentaries like a rabbi
reading Torah. "Chimes Blues"
tinkled inside glass, then took on
weight and flew, rumbled
contemplated anger, danced on top of,
danced inside the pain awhile, held
onto the light with tired arms,
then danced again, resolved
for that one moment by including
all that could not be resolved.
His face did not change; dusk-like,
the eyes were still turned inside out.

He died; the hotel closed.
It let him go a year later.
He sits inside me, bent over
like the shadowed eyes and bones
that watched those nights, and listened
while he disappeared like light.

198   FOUR FINITE SONGS:
                    AFTER RICHARD STRAUSS

1

Beside him as he dies again, you watch
the sky turn light, lighter than absence.
It is morning. The room is blurred white.
He wore tiny flowers without wrinkles.
There are icy hands around the sun. His
were so cold. The air is anxious,
wet with rain you cannot feel or see.

2

Writing this, the lines grow indistinct,
as if the letters were doubled, or ran into
each other. You have to squint to find
your own thoughts. Like words, ideas
lose their boundaries. There are so many
of them, so much to remember; clarity
torrents of mirrors, falling like rain.

3

In the parks, the people on the benches
look more and more familiar. Max and
your father playing cards; yourself hinted.
The men are wearing checkered pants,
white shoes. The shops in Florida hotels,
visiting your father; in the windows, clothes
already dead, like flowers for a funeral.

4   **199**

The last visit, the two of you holding hands
for a whole afternoon. There are certain
advantages. Forgiveness, including pain, is
sometimes clearer with duration. Your own voice
seems more worn, therefore more direct.
Love turns, like opened wine. You learn
to venerate the smell of it, emptying the glass.

ANDANTE:
AFTER A HAYDN PIANO TRIO

On the branches, strings
of icy light. At night they are

negative transparencies
floating down the dark

and falling off. The snowy farms
are fish at dawn. Gravestones

with windows that are always moving.
Summer evenings over Sortedam.

The rows of windows are distant
sounds. The soothing empty

loneliness of late June, turning
into snow. I can barely see you

in the dim bedroom, looking
at stained glass inside the cathedral,

fish buried in trees.
It is snowing on our eyes.

EXHIBITION OF AN ARTIST

You can take in the body, the flaking
reddish skin barely cramped
inside the frame. With the mirror,

you cannot tell from either side
what is reflected. Across the stomach,
the skin is stripped away; you can

watch a movie of a child being beaten
on the head by other children
at a school for eight hours straight.

The film is silent. You can look at
the hands; they have eyes and mouths
on them, are as delicate as forgiveness,

and as rough and scarred. A floodlight
glares on flashes from the mouth
and eyes. The ears dangle like forgotten

telephones. Somewhere from another mirror
in the ears, there is music; a tape recorder
playing fragments of your own singing.

BUDDY BOLDEN'S
PHOTOGRAPH

It was the picture
that started the madness.

Bolden is standing
next to Willy Cornish.

There is a white backdrop
full of grainy spackles,

paler behind the band,
as if they might fall through.

At Masonic Hall, Bolden
would bend backwards, blowing

so everyone would come
and he could bring them

together. There are cracks
in his clothes, and on

Jimmy Johnson's bass. The photo
is almost transparent. You

can look through the faces
at the charred eyes inside.

It was the light that faded
the picture. During the parade

203

with Henry Allen's band, Bolden
went mad. For twenty-four years

at East Louisiana State
Hospital, he got to look

more and more like the photograph,
the lines spreading in the sun

like tiny white wires
across his face. Perdido Street

was too far back, grainy
like the picture, a leftover

crack in his mind
he couldn't even play.

204

A PHOTOGRAPH
OF HEIDEGGER

There is no face
because he has forgotten.

The back of Heidegger
is sitting on a bench, wearing

a flat-brimmed country hat,
a folded bird waiting

for the sun. Wings down,
he listens for it

like a prayer. When
he forgot Husserl, it was

different; the sun clanged
between the trees with teasing

red of blood. He has forgotten
that light, the dark wet

clamor of rocks and rain
with faces. His shoulders sag;

there is a cane to keep
his long coat from falling

into the ground. He remembers
loss; has learned to wait for it.

Patricia Chambers Porter '62 205

Any summary of her professional career—to say
nothing of the demands of parenthood, her volunteer
activities, and other work on behalf of marginalized
people—would suggest that Patricia ("Cis") Chambers
Porter's life as a writer has been conducted in the face of
constant competition from other demands and more
urgent priorities. Yet, as she reports the ongoing
struggle to find time for writing, it is these competing
interests and commitments that provide much of what
nourishes her as a writer.

Washington, D.C., and governmental agencies and
activities have provided the focus of much of Cis
Porter's life. She has been a social worker in the District
of Columbia Welfare Department, a technical editor in
the Parliamentarian's Office on Capitol Hill, a program
specialist for the Federal Cuban-Haitian Refugee
Program, and spent 10 years in South America as a
foreign service wife. More recently, she has lived in
Tucson, Ariz., working as a grants writer for the
sanctuary movement, as a writing instructor, and as
director of volunteer services for a homeless program.
In 1993 Cis was co-founder of the Tucson Local of the
National Writers' Union.

In 1987 she completed a master of fine arts degree
in writing at George Mason University. Her poetry has
appeared in such publications as *atticus review*, *The
Alexandria Collective*, *The Federal Poet*, and *PHOEBE*.
Recently returned to the D.C. area, Cis Porter now
makes her home in Montclair, Va.

THE HALF LIFE OF VALIUM

"Take this," my mother-
in-law said, October 1967,
handing me a small blue pale tablet,
a neat line bisecting it. Where
were we? In the cafeteria
of Children's Hospital while
my son lost his voice for breath;
they carved a round hole
in his throat, popped in a metal tube,
a plunger of sorts, that day. "Eat,"
said my mother-in-law. "You must
eat." "I don't need food," I said.
She left that day. "You don't
have to go," I said.
Danny shrieked in silence, reached
baby arms to me, tears flying
it seemed, as in his pain, terror
swallowed him in silence. "Say it!"
I shouted, mouthed carefully,
"*Say* it! Mommy will understand
you!" "MOMMY!" he mouthed,
"Oh, Mommy!" and our tears
and sweat salted us both
that hot autumn day they
gave him breath for voice
and scraped away a bit
of tumor growing where
a scalpel
                could not reach.

THOMAS, AND HER
LONG HAIR HANGING DOWN

Chameleons were all the rage
when my father brought me
one, in its own white box,
a silver chain around its neck,
an alligator clip clamped to the box.

The chameleon and my father
got home late. It was morning
when, beside my oatmeal bowl,
I met Thomas, who at that moment
had not yet a name.

For the small, inquisitive creature
my delight enfolded, I chose my
father's name;
the highest tribute
for the being changing colors, magically.

My mother and I took care
of Thomas: fed him, watered him,
obtained an orb-shaped bowl from Cherry's Five and Dime—
just as the red letters on the bottom
of the white box said.

He lived awhile. I liked him,
as a child will, presuming perpetuity,
and then he was dead: stiff and strange
in his round glass bowl; unfixable.
Poor Thomas.

208

And her long hair
hanging down,
my mother cried
and weeping, said that everything died
she ever touched.

She sat on the floor,
her dark hair glistening
with morning sun.
Weeping, she sat,
her bright tears no resolution

cupping Thomas in
        her hand, and I touched the gold
upon the black
of her long hair
hanging down.

CATECHISM   **209**

The men bear weapons.
Women bear children.
Guilt's the men's burden;
Women carry hope.
Death and birth, both grieve.
Wars won, hope found: lies.

Men tell sober lies;
Play games with weapons.
The young should not grieve
(It's done for the children).
A short while grows hope,
Waylaid by the burden.

Wives share men's burden,
Permit sober lies.
They, too, would have hope,
Forget birth's weapons.
Each of us children,
Youth, age, must all grieve.

Why must we all grieve?
Not sack grief's burden?
Ah, yes. The children
Must inherit the lies.
With these as their weapons
Rout out the forces of hope.

210
Dreams live upon hope
So why do we grieve?
False are youth's weapons,
Harsh, then, youth's burden:
Joy built upon lies
Given the children.

Beggared the children,
Destroyed by their hope.
Onerous gifts, lies,
Assure that they grieve.
Theirs is the burden,
Borne on their weapons.

All children will grieve,
Find hope a burden,
In lies cloak weapons.

CAT AND WOMAN

"I Love you, Chester,"
a woman, in the short
time before dark,
after the sun has set,
allows herself to sit outside.
     She says this to her cat.
The year is 1999; the month, August.
The year is 1909; the month is August.
The year is...1955; 200 B.C..
     "I Love you," says the woman
to a small cat she has brought
with her to her Solitude: a small cat
that rises up on its toes, arches its back,
caresses the woman's hand, the better to absorb
caresses from the woman whom, whichever, the cat
relies upon, and owns.
All too often distracted, preoccupied, lost
to the neural and tangible world
around her thereabout;
what about—?
     ...What is the error, the air, the timing of
events,
the tuning of hours, the turning of affairs, that
permits her to lift high the cat,
which has followed her after she has loosed it:
to find out-of-doors that essential particles conjoin
as they meet?

212

FOR MY SON
(on February 22, 1979)

"All you ever do is read; read and type,"
my son just said. No, Son, my David, not quite.
I sleep a lot in daytime, when you are home.
You are on to something, though, and in your
eight years' wisdom, found a way to say it.
Catch. I hide from you.
These pretenses, these Victorian takings to the bed,
allow me midnight life. Am I one weird Dracula, Son,
who leaves you bleeding, transformed by the absence of
a touch, a time, for you? Do you yearn for me as I fear
        to ache for you?

Have you not been invited for a walk with me
and preferred the squawking birds and surly
ruffians, Tasmanian devils of that little box
I bought you so you could watch gentle father figures
and British drama? And, if I am honest, escape
from you again? Do you watch so ardently, not t.v. but
        me, reading my
close fear in my unspoken denials, trying to win my
        arms, denying me?
Can your intuition be so piercing? Yes. You are eight
        and wise.
You know my frightened subterfuges, my hidden
love for you better, David, Son, than do I.

HERA TO GAEA

Hera, tender of fire, practiced housewifery, dazed by
    time's passage,
the growth of the children, the flames' variant shapes as
    she boiled
water, broiled lamb, served feasts, ate alone,
waited for Zeus to come home.

Dozing, Hera roused, amazed, a bee sting prick
to her back. Startled, she touched warm wet
blood at her breast; turned,
saw shadowed Zeus retreat, rapier just
sheathed. She did not ask why; lord
knows, men have their reasons, even gods.

Trouble-eyed, the last cat from child's play hopped to
    Hera's lap, licked
blood and salt, questioned her, forepaws on her
    shoulders, forehead to
her eyes. Hera stroked
the old cat's pelt and felt, finally, at last,
the pain of an unsafe house.

Hera rocked the cat for old time's sake
till its purr rumbled through old bones,
slack flesh; set the small prowler
on the hearth, stoked the fire, moving slow
with sorrow and her age. Something in her
stirred toward rage.

Firmly, Hera claimed the cruet flame; stepped
into night and fled, winter firefly blinking

214

light. Tender of fire, Hera pierced bluest
dark, illumined rocks, mouse holes, owl eyes,
bats, moss, bark; bobbing, charting her erratic
course not from but toward–.

She couldn't name her destination; only knew her
flame must reach it; thorns clawed her skirt.
Stubble stabbed her feet. Iron cold
caused her bones to throb.

Hera staggers with her bowl of flaming household
oil: beeswax, spermaceti, wick; stumbles, lifts
high her chalice, drops. Wax, flames,
cascade, consume her.

A half-grown girl-child, abandoned, Gaea
sleeps in a stone shed at forest's edge;
wakes to crackling, strange scent, and light.
Puzzled, Gaea touches earthen floor, tiptoes to
the juncture where wood meets field. From earth-
pyred Hera, heat fingers cast clear shadows.
Stunned, the child stares.

At dawn, Gaea crushes hoarfrost underfoot;
furtive, bold, responding to a dream sensed, not
named; claims the cruet, its flame blue guttering.
      Gagging, driven,
Gaea gathers tallow from the wick
of Hera, rekindles the household torch.

Tracking singed twigs, wax spattered rocks,
Gaea retraces Hera's route.

Stephen Brooks '64   215

Steve Brooks, who now writes under the name Stephen Abhaya, has had a career that is both original and representative of his generation. He came to Grinnell from Moline, Ill.; after graduation he taught school for three years then entered the M.A. program in poetry at San Francisco State. In the '70s, he was active in the flourishing coffeehouse poetry-reading scene and published a sequence of poems and drawings, *Philip Blanc in San Francisco* (Panjandrum Press, 1972). Later some of his work appeared with that of four other Bay Area poets in a volume titled *Five on the Western Edge* (Momo's Press, 1976).

Travels in India and a meeting with the teacher called Papaji have had a strong influence on his creative work as both poet and visual artist. He now lives in Seattle and produces his poetry (which he often illustrates) under the "Fearless Books" imprint. Recent titles include *On Milk Island, Death, The Vigil of Homeward Bound*, and a "zenictionary of zeniversal zenguage" called *Zencabulary*. He is co-author (with Joan Amby) of a textbook, *Sex in All Our Lives: Creating a Personal Journal* (1999).

No small selection from his poems can very truly represent Stephen Abhaya (Brooks). He is best read in the bulk, for his total work—a kind of ongoing Song of Myself—offers to my inZENsitive mind the picture of something like a generous pudding containing more than a few crunchy nuts and plump raisins. One is

216

repeatedly coming across tidbits—splendid verbal gestures, phrases, images, rounded utterances—as good as this one:

> In full song, lying back
> against the mountain range,
> one arm along the crest ridge,
> the other, pulling the wind closer.
> ("Three," *Sonnets to Rilke*)

Steve has responded at different times to poets as dissimilar as Keats, Robinson Jeffers, and Galway Kinnell; it's probably fair to see in him a kinship to the Beat Poets, and behind them Walt Whitman looms in the distance. But he reports that when his mother read over his work she told him, "Stephen, I don't know where you came from." To which Steve's answer— "Neither do I"—might as well stand as the last word.

PHILIP BLANC
WAS READING A BOOK

I am the author of this book, he said.
I am the pages. I am the cover.

He ran through the print
until he was exhausted
and covered with ink.

He swam between the lanes of words.
He climbed onto the sentences
and ran across them.

He ran across rows of desks
in school, laughing.

He looked at the book,
the size of his hand.

I was a good boy once, he said,
but now I am everything.

218   STANDING ON FISHES

My friend, Peter, who I always thought
was another swimmer, declared he'd
rather have been a wrestler or a gymnast.

Instead, he swam, because he liked the coach.
I've always had trouble with authority, he said.

Of course, I thought, his wiry compression,
explosive temperament, a grappling wrestler,
or a bounding gymnast, but not a supple,
half-drowner like me.

He would not take instruction inside his capability.
He grew to despise the water, but then, so did I,
after five years. Five years of wrestling the water,
bounding across it like a stone.

It took many more years to sink,
to take the chance of dissolving,

To stand up on myself,
like Jesus upon the fishes.

THE ETERNAL RUSE   **219**

I want you to be mine, and I want
to be yours, and every time I say that,
I want us to laugh at our little ruse.

I want us to merge into one, and every time
I say that, I want us to laugh at our little ruse.

I want us to walk down Paris boulevards
and forget who we are and what we're doing
and where we're going, and then we can laugh
at our little ruse.

I want you to be here because you are part
of me and I am part of you, and the hardest
laugh is to laugh alone at our little ruse.

Being so far apart for so long a time,
learning all we can about the perfect
and the imperfect in the world,
where learning to be without
is a greater ruse
than any we could play together,
or on each other.

Knowing the ruse of life
and loving the ruse in its face,
the eternal ruse of realities
and the ruse of all the rest.

220

I SPILLED COFFEE
ON THE BUDDHA

I was respectful,
listening to the Buddha.

My body was vibrating,
a small, constant tremor.
I felt humble, a little afraid.

The Buddha's words were sweet,
a gentle breeze in soft sun.
I reached for my coffee,
and in a broken moment,
I spilled coffee on the Buddha.

Without innocence and without guilt,
my fingers knocked against the lip of the cup.

I looked up, horrified.
My devil of a heart was laughing,
and the Buddha was gone.

In his place, in the doorway,
was a chubby family of hungry patrons,
entering the ordinary cafe.

A MAN
SHOUTS DESIRE

A man
shouts desire
from a car.

Ooh! Yeah!

A blind cow
walks into
a tree.

The bird
on the cow's back
sings.

222   THE VIGIL OF THE HOMEWARD BOUND

To the woman nearby, to the baker,
to my son, to my daughter, I want to
tell you how grateful I am, when the poet
in me is awakened by the poem in me, and
I want to cry for the vigil I keep, when I am
away from this way All of Life makes itself
known to me, and I welcome what welcomes
me most alive, what only I can do, what I don't
do, because, in the doing of it I am nothing but
what it is, it is my doing and my undoing, in my
homecoming, I cry for homelessness and for
the homeward bound.

Paul Jenkins '64   223

Poems by Paul Jenkins have appeared in *The New Yorker*, *Paris Review*, *Gettysburg Review*, *Kenyon Review*, and many other places. To date he has published two books of poetry, *Forget the Sky* (1980) and *Radio Tooth* (1997), which won the Award Series Prize, selected by Alberto Ríos. A third book, *Six Small Fires*, is due to come out in 2001. Currently, he teaches poetry and poetry writing at Hampshire College and is poetry editor and general editor of *The Massachusetts Review*.

Paul Jenkins is a poet of startlingly apt likenesses and uncomfortably bold reflections, in language fine and scrupulous. There is nothing wayward about his avoidance of conventional punctuation. That feature of the poems here lends added weight to the carefully judged line and stanza breaks and coaxes the reader into a more alert, more "open" involvement in the poem's way of meaning.

224   THIS HORSE

Muzzle like a shoe on a shoe last
Legs like cocked rifles
And they say the miracle's not the body but the soul

Into that oblong sheath
Slips a dagger of thought
As out from its gaze it bursts into full stride

Now it lingers at the far end of the field
Neck down nose down
A magnified flea

When I draw close it looks up
An entire orchestra poised for the downbeat
My own chest the drum

Thudding and repeating
It's got your number you don't have a clue
And

This horse is real
Unlike us whose glory will have been
We longed to exist beyond ourselves

OCTOBER

When my legs are bald as an egg when I mistake my
daughter
For my mother I will not be serene I'll argue with the
doctors
And lurch in and out of clarity like a radio in a storm

Cricket behind the bookcase it's my hard time of year
When the light hangs glassy when the maples let go
And the far ridge bristles like a banner in Arabic

Remember childhood when the world was obvious as
an apple
And the grownups lingered talking behind their hands
No we were never innocent not even then

Inside the wall something rustles like a stage curtain
Then claws at the sheetrock as if a mineshaft had
collapsed
And suddenly I'm holding onto life by my teeth

ANTIETAM

Now that everyone's father is/was alcoholic
And the two Germanies merge at midnight like a woods
I refuse to be healed I refuse to love my neighbor
Or embrace the one true church like a boy his dog

You could see them camped on either bank of the stream
Under paper hats as if tomato seedlings might freeze
Is it true what Davis thought of Lincoln
A lost calf bawling for its ma

In the name of union in the name of stand or fall
And the creek a midline between a brain's two lobes
And the bridge two thousand went to cross in waves
And all the hillside a storm surf of debris

How I detest the mathematics the language the snapping flags
The premise of oneness that passes for wisdom even now
As if the manic-depressive were a plot against the good
And the cross-dresser and the lotused self-immolator

Now that all our violence has lodged itself within
Like a fishbone in the windpipe or been exported overseas
So that innocence may survive innocence and the dream
Of the time we fought it out in the open and were made whole

BLEEDING-HEART

The blossoms are the disease
I love the purple nubs punching through leaf mould
And the crown that widens like an ottoman sofa
And the toothy trinitarian leaves
Like a raccoon's pawprints puddled with chlorophyl
When out of nowhere a slender arm ramps out
And eleven tiny lockets nod into being
Eleven soccer jerseys in graduating size
Bending a clothesline if only I had a family
This large I could field an entire team
By the next day eleven fat pink notes
Hang from the stave of an illuminated manuscript
And the day after that Khmer Rouge single-file
Emerge from the undergrowth shivering in broad daylight
While eleven mild Jesuses bare their chests
Nearly translucent with a garnet crumb inside
Exactly the way the X-ray's cloud-
Map darkened suddenly at the center
And two months later Ruth was dead
It's the way they tiptoe from stage right
Eleven sugar-plum fairies in matching tutus
That has me stringing this necklace of *ands*
On a thin thread of nothing
Or the way death's enjoying a growth-spurt of late
And my mind's gone a little haywire
Go ahead ask me
As spring keeps replaying its Lazarus-note
Like the boy who found crude crosses on a hill
Behind the uncle's house where three dogs lay buried

228   And simply listened in silence to everything has
       Its own time to be born and to die and then
       Said let's just dig them up

"SEARCH GOES ON FOR MISSING WOMAN" **229**
–Cape Cod Times headline

I have sobbed on an airplane but I have never been
    distraught
I held Ellen all day then she held me for two
As we wept non-stop over a private matter
All right fifteen-minute spurts disheartened but not
    distraught
When they put Mona Foster in a ward I was nearly ten
She had the tannest legs of my parents' circle
Was she sick of playing golf
Had she never been to the county fair
The day two men working behind glass
Carve a life-size cow out of a huge loaf of butter
Couldn't anybody make her laugh
A blue minivan stands outside the watchful diner
Awaiting the woman whose keys and a note
Are hand-delivered to a husband in a beachfront rental
The children off poking at sandcrabs with brooms
Who reads and rereads the passage that ends
You'll all be better off without me
The hostess listens to the officer's sketch
No no one by that description
A search team plies the dunes a dive team the bay
I can hear the what what of the helicopter's rotor
She doesn't want to be found she wants to make for thin air
Let me try and find her
I'm camping up the road I'm a father with a child
I'm a boomerang lost in dream-time I'm a beanbag with
    a hole
And I'm sick of grief's turning intelligible in the end

230   Here's where she stopped to pee on the sawgrass
Here's where she stripped and began brushing away the marks
Here's where a seal said slip inside my coat
Before she resurfaced in Rio in a red spaghetti-strap dress
Forgive my shallow imagination
When I think of suicide my mind turns to mist
What is dailiness to the distraught
A stock truck jammed with cattle
A lightbulb that pops and all that's left are the seeds
A spiderweb brushing your lips in the basement
If I find her in time will she consent to live
I'll say what can be so bad
I'll say how about I order a basket of clam strips
And a bottle of Ron Rico and we'll see what's next
I'll say no more shit
I'll say you sound like you deserve a little vacation
I know a place they will never think to look
With their want and their hope and their gluey hands
I'll say no one saves another
I'll say everything I can

ORNETTIANA

Yesterday I was going on sixteen
Thumbing beneath her waistband neither of us disrobing
This morning in the mirror I'm eighty-one
Silver tufts of hair escaping my left earlobe
Last night steeped in the old broth
I woke to a bear beneath me in a tree
Who smelled like green steak and an oil refinery
And woke again lugging a dead arm across my chest
Until it woke all by its lonesome
I lied about sixteen I was twenty-seven or fifty-five
Before my body caught on to its own sheer pleasure
The same year Montana relifted its speed limit
Now in two seconds flat I'm standing in Brazil
All it takes is a word
And the color of the voice returns exactly
Come five thousand miles and nine winters in the ground
To find me aimless in eucalyptus
The years between overlapping like starlight
Past lives please spare me as it is
I'll never finish this one if I make it to a hundred
Lindbergh in the fourth-grade reader as remote
As a pygmy on the Congo now my near contemporary
Only a generation and a stray thought away
As July the lavish the extreme
Senses the night hours lengthen and buttons up its sleeves
Fat green houseflies bumping against my ankles
Will time ever die I confess
I am not a strong person I am a very weak person
Anything passes through me

232   As the dream-hours melt into morning's stream
           Cornbread to Cambodia back to her cotton underpants
           Next Thursday and last Monday Free Jazz in the park
           So all-at-once the drummer sits nodding in wonder
           Time who has the inner life of a twig
           And the saxophones like horses that have thrown their riders
           And me every age I am

Mark Schorr '66

An avid and selfless student, practitioner, and advocate of poetry–and indeed of many another worthy cause–might fairly, but not adequately, characterize Mark Schorr for those who knew him at Grinnell and have kept abreast of his career from Harvard graduate student to prep school teacher to professional computer whiz and tireless worker for a productive accommodation between information technology and the humanities.

Since Mark's first published poem appeared in the *Paris Review*, the year he moved to Andover, Mass., he has participated in workshops, group readings, and local anthologies, and on the board of the Robert Frost Festival in Lawrence, Mass. He devotes much of his time to producing hand-printed chapbooks containing his work and broadsides celebrating the visits to Andover of such notable poets as Allen Ginsberg, Amy Clampitt '41, Donald Hall, Jane Kenyon, and Seamus Heaney. He has also helped translate into English the works of several Russian and one Cuban poet and has served as editor of *The Andover Anthology*, published in *The Bridge*, an Internet-based poetry journal.

Mark is a maker and a preserver of connections– such as that between Andover, his present home, and an Iowa college founded by missionaries from Andover Seminary and now called Grinnell, or that between his birthplace, Chicago, and the various other places whose cultures have enriched that beautiful city.

234

GRAFFITI

Thinking about your latest letter, I hear Canada geese
proclaiming their neighborly rights to head for
the nearest pond. It needs to be cleaned up
Internet, my computer neighborhood, fares not much better.
Vandals trashed my site last night, it wasn't working
for a day or longer. If that sounds like sour grapes,
it wasn't. I think of what's posted there as hardly
something more than scrawls above a phone booth
while waiting for a number. Graffiti, yes,
but certainly no Basquiat. Yet enough good reasons
to explore the public realm by negation.
For every thousand hours of broadband
Disneyfied animation pointcast o'er land and ocean,
a one-minute sonnet pipes through hollow reeds.

BEAUTIFUL CITY

Beautiful city, from which I came.
Forever amber, I cannot show my friend
the sweep of your broadbacked spacious skies—
from the fetal heartbeat of your R&B
or the illuminations of your armillary bridges
from the clean sweep of your inland sea
or the glacial basement of your middlewestern land
as varied as your facebricked one-acre prairie lots
or your recycled synagogues of iron-columned gesso,
and your integrated neighborhoods that stay just so
and minarets that call me to pray among you,
in lion-porched and roof-shimmered art palaces
in rock-ribbed and granite-trussed Monadnocks,
beautiful city, always changing in my mind,
defining that which can not be defined.

236

BABI YAR AFTER 10 YEARS
for Everett Gendler

It has been too long since we have talked
about the walk around that place outside Kiev
where so much happened we would just as soon
had not—but even there imagining the worst
and hardly a monument or official sign of comfort
except the ravens circling the ditches kept
no more than scythed and in their bulldozed state
where brigades moved and decisions once were made.
And I remember how you passed me on the path
until another man, Bruce, caught up with us,
a big man who worked in the mill from eighteen on,
and, without saying anything, the three of us
embraced as if to say, this is a century,
this is a place someone will try to wish away
unless we remember it here and mourn forever.

KANSAS VORTEX

after Ginsberg's Wichita Vortex *and in memory
of my Grandfather, Max Schorr, 1858–1918*

Pardon, old father, if I tell others how
you fell into the vortex of Kansas and all America
without knowing about how your family would fall free
without knowing when and where the Messiah would come–
but not knowing any more likely place than one not far
from where you landed in the wide broad rolling earthy vortex
and without knowing the American poet-prophet Ginsberg
who would speak from this cynosure not just to heal
wounds of unjust wars but of the whole American language
then taxed by war and who could have imagined that
from Ellis Island point of disembarkation
from Hebrew immigrant aid certification
where but in the belly and the breasts of Kansas
who would have guessed all the names that would pour forth
everlasting allah kir christ nirvannah buddha elohim?

238

AT THE UNIVERSITY OF
FORT HARE, SOUTH AFRICA
for Christopher Shaw

If, after all that has happened,
the pass books, the razor-wire, and arrests,
that violate the premises of this place,
the open letters, "When...in the name of God..."
the arrests taking place on the premises;
if after all that has happened,
there is still water that splashes
from an open well, like language,
clear, unpolluted, and without banalities;
if there are still ideas, multifaceted,
as the clay fired where pavement bricks
still reveal those who arranged them;
Then, despite the uses of adversity,
there still can be–a University.

TO THE END OF TIME

In the concentrated rage of camps one sound man
Olivier Messiaen noted and in the first camp light
heard thrushes under sirens strained vibrato.
As the day progressed, he found against
the screeching of arriving trains, a nightingale.

Winding through the alternating currents of tired
generators to the abyss of birds, *ses tristesses,*
ses lassitudes, les oiseaux, he found in them
the opposite of time–its jubilant rainbow voice.

Even those tortured can hear the open
tones of doves if they do not give up.
So we have to the end of time, this journey,
muted, punctuated as much by sounds
that are without the camp as those within
and time ends only with their announcement.

240   *Robert Heidbreder '69*

Most of us have a double relation to children's poetry:
It remains a vivid and sustaining memory from our
own childhood, and there is also the pleasure it gives us
as we read it to our children. For over 25 years Robert
Heidbreder has been engaged with children's verse, both
as a teacher of kindergarten and grades one and two in
the public schools of Vancouver, Canada, and as an
author–well-known in Canada and becoming so in the
United States–of poems for children. "Poetry," he says,
"has been the glue, the essential sticky stuff, that has
held my teaching and my classes together."

Along with his duties as a teacher, Robert often gives
readings in schools, libraries, and at children's literary
festivals, participates in poetry workshops, and lectures in
both Canada and the United States on poetry in relation
to reading and language development.

Heidbreder majored in classical languages and
literature at Grinnell, where he was elected to Phi Beta
Kappa, then did graduate work in classics at the
University of Washington. In 1970 he emigrated to
Canada and continued his graduate studies at the
University of British Columbia, eventually shifting
from classics to the teacher education program. In 1975
he became a Canadian citizen.

His first book of children's poems, *Don't Eat
Spiders*, was published by the Oxford University Press
in 1975. Since its success, Heidbreder's poems have
appeared in numerous anthologies and in such publica-

tions as *Ladybug Magazine*. His latest books are *Eenie* **241**
Meenie Manitoba (1996), *Python Play* (1999), and *I*
Wished for a Unicorn (2000).

Beneath the beguiling surface of Robert
Heidbreder's work, one senses a firm identity and
purpose, a "deep and cherished commitment to Canada
as a country and as a state of mind, to giving children a
language-rich and playful environment, and to the
limitless possibilities of public education."

DON'T EAT SPIDERS

Daddy said to me,
"Don't eat spiders,
Don't you dare.
They may be delicious,
But I don't care.
Don't eat spiders
Alive or dead.
Don't eat spiders,
That's what I said.
Don't eat spiders
Even in play,
Fried or mashed
Or *any* way.
Don't eat spiders,
That's what I say.
Never, ever,
That's what I say!"

But I answered Daddy,
"Tell my why!
Will I get sick?
Will I die?
I'll eat spiders,
I don't care.
I'll eat spiders
On a dare."

I ate a spider
Off the ground.
I swallowed a spider,
It wriggled around.

243

SUD-DEN-LY…
I grew eight legs,
They're skinny and hairy.
I shrank to a spider,
Creepy and scary.
I sit in a web,
I eat dead flies,
I watch the world
With eight beady eyes.

So don't eat spiders,
I hope you see,
Unless you want to be
A spider like me.
 And don't eat spiders.
Do you see?
Cause if you eat spiders
You might eat ME!

244   COPYCAT

Copycat, copycat,
Shadow's a copycat!

Out in the sun
Whenever I run,
It runs.
Whenever I twirl,
It twirls.
I curl up small.
It curls up small.
I stand up tall.
It stands up tall.

Copycat, copycat,
Shadow's a copycat.

Whenever I hide,
It hides.
I spread out wide.
It spreads out wide.
I pat my head.
It pats its head.
I fall down dead.
It falls down dead.

But when I go inside to stay,
Copycat, copycat goes away!

TODAY AND YESTERDAY

The wind blew hard
It blew me away
It blew me back to yesterday
It blew tomorrow to today
It blew today to yesterday
It blew me to this day behind
It blew me to another time

Now I'm stuck in yesterday
And there I guess I'll have to stay
Until it blows me back away
Until it blows me to today

246   PEPPERMINT MOOSE

A ginger sheep	(clap your hands twice)
And a nutmeg mare	(tap your shoulders twice)
Danced all night	(roll your hands around each other)
With a cinnamon bear	(roll your hands again)
The cinnamon bear	(clap your hands twice)
And a cardamom goose	(tap your shoulders twice)
Played all day	(thump your thighs for a running moose sound)
With a peppermint moose.	(thump your thighs again)

THE FASTEST RUNNER

I leap across all hurdles.
    I sprint upon my hands.
I dash along sea beaches
    on scorching summer sands.
I shoot up icy mountains
    in grueling winter freeze.
I speed past roaring rivers
    like a cyclone in the trees.
I take on every challenge.
    I win at every race.
Oh, I'm the fastest runner,
    I'm sheer energy and grace.
Yes, I'm the fastest runner,
    all my friends and foes agree,
When my imagination
    runs away with me.

PYTHON PLAY

Keep your eye out for a python,
  sneaking 'round to meet you,
  peeking through the waving grass,
  sleeking up to greet you.

Keep your eye out for this python,
  its darting tongue can tease you,
  its slapping, wrapping body could
  just slip around and squeeze you.

If you spot this python,
  this and not another,
  don't yell for help,
  don't faint away,
  it's just my reptile BROTHER!
  He loves his silly python—
  he says it's so fantastic!
  And I promised not to tell
  but...

  SHHHHHHHHshhhh!...
  it's only plastic.

River Malcolm '69

Under her given name, Molly Malcolm made her mark
upon Grinnell of the late '60s–the Grinnell of social
activism and protest movements. "I felt an overwhelm-
ing need to contribute to peace and justice in the
world," she writes of herself in that period. "Changing
my name to River was part of a long process of
accepting and learning to find beauty in the world,
despite its imperfections. ... My name adds a little
poetry to my daily life, and poetry has helped me to
stay alive." Having majored in mathematics, she did
graduate work in that field at the University of Wiscon-
sin and later studied molecular biology at M.I.T., then
electrical engineering and creative writing at San Diego
State University. This educational odyssey is matched
by the voyage of discovery that has been her work
experience–cleaning houses, painting, modeling for life
drawing classes, renovating buildings, printing, and
technical writing. With the completion of a master's
degree in counseling from S.D.S.U., these two journeys
converged in a career in counseling and family therapy.
She now lives on Orcas Island (in the state of Washing-
ton) with her partner of 17 years, writes, pursues her
professional practice, and walks her dog daily in the
woods around Cascade Lake.

River Malcom's poetry has appeared in *Calyx,
Claiming the Spirit Within, The Real Woman Millen-
nium 2000 Calendar,* and numerous self-published
chapbooks.

THE TWO GODDESSES

PERSEPHONE

At first it was only the lily
a kind of annunciation
as when Gabriel held it
singing birth birth birth
but that was another story.
     I bent to pick it, that lily,
and in that moment
was blessed: was at one
with the garland of girls
that danced in the meadow.
Softer than petals,
the blue up above,
the sun's bright caress.
Softer than petals,
the swirl of their skirts,
the brush of their maiden flesh.

     And then the earth opened.
Seized by a tremor of darkness
and wrenched from the world I'd known,
darkness forced into my mouth
and between my teeth,
darkness thrust down my throat,
darkness thrust through my nose,
darkness thrust through my ears,
darkness forced into my eyes,
a fist of darkness between my thighs
tearing my insides,

and knowing

    I was forever changed
    forever different.
So it was Hades I wed,
King of Death,
God of the world below.

And where was my mother, oh goddess of all things
    that grow,
when his rough hands pulled me down to the root of
    it all?
Where was my mother and what was her power
    then,
when Hades took me like a calf or a dog or a bench
and made me a thing, a possession of his?
Where was my mother then, and where the dance of
    her golden grains?

    Do not
    talk to me about life and the living.
I am the wife of Hades,
I am His Queen.
The shades salute him, and I,
seated on the cold gold throne at his side,
I too am saluted.
Before me, as before him,
the Underworld bows.
At my every word now,
the Nether World cringes
and scurries to obey.
Even Cerberus the fierce

252

whines when I approach, and begs
for a pat from his mistress's hand.

As for me, I do not think
of my mother's soft eyes,
her bosom, her arms,
they are part of a life I have left,
torn from me by the dark.
Where was she
when the earth opened up
and swallowed my girlhood?

And now I am Queen.
I have grown somewhat fond of my power.
Do not think I partake innocently.
Do not think I mistake these pomegranate seeds.
I know they're the food of the dead:
seeds of power, seeds of blood.
I who was torn from the world of my mother
I know these seeds.
Before that moment, there was no force in my world,
life danced in my mother's sweet circles
of flowers and fruits, growing and grains,
but now things are different.
I'm frankly intrigued by the taste of command
and savor the ruby red seeds slowly
crushing them knowingly
between strong teeth no longer innocent.
It is Hades, my husband, who bids me cease,
knowing,
as those of my father's generation

do know,
that Destiny must be obeyed
even by gods.

And I go
as if I could be again the same girl I was,
soft skin soft small bosom soft eyes,
I, Queen of Death, Lady of Darkness,
I who rise from the earth
as the lily once did
as if to return to those innocent dances,
as if to rejoin that garland of girls,
as if my mother and I could be reunited,
as if the two goddesses could be made one.
She who blesses the earth with abundance,
she for whom flowers, grains, fruits grow once again,
she is my mother.
And I am her daughter, I,
in whom seeds of death are planted
and will sprout.

DEMETER

From the other side of the world child
I heard your scream
felt your abduction
in every pore of my skin
the stench of your violation,
the core of your sacred body defiled,
darkness forcing itself deep inside,
knowing I never prepared you for this.

254

Only the Sun would name the perpetrator,
but I should have known
who else could it be
but your father (his brother, what difference?):
male gods who long ago usurped
the power of our grandmothers,
those great ancient goddesses,
who being keepers of life
could not deny the gods their destiny.
I too, daughter, I am a keeper of life,
though while separate from you
I forget the world placed in my keeping.

And I mourn.
Nothing grows.
I reward small human kindnesses
and dream of giving immortality to a human child
as if somehow that would undo the harm
from which I could not preserve you.
But destiny, laughing, terrifies its mother
to intervene, and I a goddess
cannot do even this one small deed.
And I mourn.
Earth is barren, humans starve
baffled by this drama of the gods.

Daughter, do not imagine I deceive myself
or dream I can call you back as you were.
Nor do I dream of freeing you,
when you think of my absence, my failure,
from the hatred that hardens your eyes.

How can a goddess who makes the very grain to grow   **255**
allow her own child to be raped?

Do not be afraid: I know of your hate.
Even the goddesses, especially the goddesses
must dance with destiny, daughter.
Do not think I require you back as you were,
I know you are changed.
And I too, daughter, I also am changed,
oh flesh of my flesh,
these seeds of death within you,
they are seeds in my flesh.

I embrace all of you, daughter,
the change and the hate,
the longing to partake of your violator's power,
and I call you, I call you forth as you are
knowing you may not be able to love me now
in the face of my failed power,
power that seemed so great
to your child eyes.

You will never know Persephone
except as you rest your brow on my bosom
and remember a little
the girl you once were
and how we were whole
you will never know
the joy I feel in your being
no matter where you go
no matter what seeds of death sprout in you

256

no matter how pregnant with winter
oh my sweet flower of spring
you will never know
how my love for you makes the grains grow.

THE WOMAN WHO
WALKED ON WATER

It wasn't the water really
She never really wanted
to walk on water.
It was that she wanted somehow
to touch the horizon:
that outstretched edge of the ocean
edge of her limited human vision, edge
of her passing day.

She dreamed of walking
barefoot through the vanishing rose
and apricot glow of the absent sun,
of giving herself to the colors, one
with the edge of all she had ever loved.

She hardly noticed her feet
touching the sea's supple surface,
or that it supported her weight,
so that for the flutter of an eyelid,
the pause before a heartbeat,

she failed to sink.

LOOKING FOR MY FIRST KITTEN

Before I met you, what
were you doing? Walking the sky,
lapping the Milky Way? Is that why
your fur crackles with night,
your paws trail moonlight,
stars smear your face?
Is that why the green
of another world invites
through your eyes? Why the waves
of your pleasure rub against mine
until even the lack in me
stretches and purrs?

Edward Hirsch '72

No one knows better than Ed Hirsch the grinding effort and pure joy of a lifelong commitment to poetry: absorbing it, learning to write it, teaching it to others, and writing about it both as a boundless study and a careful art. As an undergraduate from North Side Chicago, Hirsch already knew poetry was his calling and (thanks to the good offices of Grinnell's president, Glenn Leggett) took one of his college semesters in the Writers' Workshop at the University of Iowa. Then, reversing the field, he returned to Grinnell to resume his collegiate football career and was named an Academic All-American in that sport. After Grinnell, Ed spent a year abroad studying poetry on a Watson Fellowship, then earned a Ph.D. in folklore at the University of Pennsylvania.

Poems, critical essays, reviews, and other writings by Edward Hirsch frequently appear in this country's leading intellectual and artistic journals. He has published five books of poems: *For the Sleepwalkers* (1981), *Wild Gratitude* (1986), *The Night Parade* (1989), *Earthly Measures* (1994), and *On Love* (1998). He has also published two prose books: *How to Read a Poem and Fall in Love with Poetry* (1999) and *Responsive Reading* (1999). He writes a regular column on poetry for the *American Poetry Review*, serves as the editorial adviser in poetry for *DoubleTake*, and teaches in the Creative Writing Program at the University of Houston.

260   A handful of his poems is no adequate sampling of Ed Hirsch's work–the scope of its subject matter, its full-throttle intensity and intellectual voracity, the daring and resourcefulness with which it accepts the challenges of form. His many awards and distinctions include the National Book Critics Circle Award (for *Wild Gratitude*), a Guggenheim Fellowship, the Prix de Rome, and an American Academy of Arts and Letters Award for Literature. In 1998 he received a MacArthur Fellowship.

IN SPITE OF EVERYTHING,
THE STARS

Like a stunned piano, like a bucket
of fresh milk flung into the air
or a dozen fists of confetti
thrown hard at a bride
stepping down from the altar,
the stars surprise the sky.
Think of dazed stones
floating overhead, or an ocean
of starfish hung up to dry. Yes,
like a conductor's expectant arm
about to lift toward the chorus,
or a juggler's plates defying gravity,
or a hundred fastballs fired at once
and freezing in midair, the stars
startle the sky over the city.

And that's why drunks leaning up
against abandoned buildings, women
hurrying home on deserted side streets,
policemen turning blind corners, and
even thieves stepping from alleys
all stare up at once. Why else do
sleepwalkers move toward the windows,
or old men drag flimsy lawn chairs
onto fire escapes, or hardened criminals
press sad foreheads to steel bars?
Because the night is alive with lamps!
That's why in dark houses all over the city
dreams stir in the pillows, a million
plumes of breath rise into the sky.

262   DAYS OF 1968

She walked through Grant Park during the red days of summer.
One morning she woke up and smelled tear gas in her hair.

She liked Big Brother and the Holding Company, Bob Dylan,
Sly & the Family Stone, The Mothers of Invention.

When Jimi Hendrix played Purple Haze in a Jam Session
she had a vision of the Trail of Tears and the Cherokee Nation.

She dropped acid assiduously for more than a year.
She sang, "I want to take you higher and higher,"

and dreamt of cleansing the doors of perception.
After she joined the Sky Church I never saw her again...

Days of 1968, sometimes your shutters open
and I glimpse a star gleaming in the constellations.

I can almost reach up and snag her by the hand.
I can go to her if I don't look back at the ground.

COLETTE

My mother used to say, "Sit down, dear,
and don't cry. The worst thing for a woman
is her first man—the one who kills you.
After that, marriage becomes a long career."
Poor Sido! She never had another career
and she knew first-hand how love ruins you.
The seducer doesn't care about his woman,
even as he whispers endearments in her ear.

Never let anyone destroy your inner spirit.
Among all the forms of truly absurd courage
the recklessness of young girls is outstanding.
Otherwise there would be far fewer marriages
and even fewer affairs that overwhelm marriages.
Look at me: it's amazing I'm still standing
after what I went through with ridiculous courage.
I was made to suffer, but no one broke my spirit.

Every women wants her adventure to be a feast
of ripening cherries and peaches, Marseilles figs,
hot-house grapes, champagne shuddering in crystal.
Happiness, we believe, is on sumptuous display.
But unhappiness writes a different kind of play.
The gypsy gazes down into a clear blue crystal
and sees rotten cherries and withered figs.
Trust me: loneliness, too, can be a feast.

Ardor is delicious, but keep your own room.
One of my husbands said: is it impossible

264

for you to write a book that isn't about love,
adultery, semi-incestuous relations, separation?
(Of course, this was before our own separation.)
He never understood the natural law of love,
the arc from the possible to the impossible...
I have extoled the tragedy of the bedroom.

We need exact descriptions of the first passion,
so pay attention to whatever happens to you.
Observe everything: love is greedy and forgetful.
By all means fling yourself wildly into life
(though sometimes you will be flung back by life)
but don't let experience make you forgetful
and be surprised by everything that happens to you.
We are creative creatures fuelled by passion.

One final thought about the nature of love.
Freedom should be the first condition of love
and work is liberating (*a novel about love
cannot be written while you are making love*).
Never underestimate the mysteries of love,
the eminent dignity of not talking about love.
Passionate attention is prayer, prayer is love.
Savor the world. Consume the feast with love.

IOWA FLORA   **265**
(In Memory of Amy Clampitt)

We thought we were having an indigenous childhood
splashed with Indian paintbrush and grassy knolls
thickened by birdfoot violets and ordinary goldenrod,

but we kept finding noxious alien weeds in the hills–
quackgrass and thistle, European morning glory
that no state legislation could control.

We inherited pioneer grasses high as a prairie
schooner, but there were also fresh settlements
of bog flowers and refugees from the sea–

coast marshes, silky-leaved Virginia plants
and Texas marigolds, imported seeds and ornamentals,
weeds from the wasted villages of other continents.

Nature consists of immigrants and mongrels:
you showed us how to prize coincidence and impurity
in wayward fields, the deserted and marginal…

I went down to the swamp to mourn for you, Amy,
and it was as if Providence led me to the place
where I stumbled upon yellow swamp betony

and pink foxglove mingled with something nameless
(*unfathomable the mystery before us*, you said)
and the shining, cup-flowered grass of Parnassus.

OCEAN OF GRASS

The ground was holy, but the wind was harsh
and unbroken prairie stretched for hundreds of miles
so that all she could see was an ocean of grass.

Some days she got so lonely she went outside
and nestled among the sheep, for company.
The ground was holy, but the wind was harsh

and prairie fires swept across the plains,
lighting up the country like a vast tinderbox
until all she could see was an ocean of flames.

She went three years without viewing a tree.
When her husband finally took her on a timber run
she called the ground holy and the wind harsh

and got down on her knees and wept inconsolably,
and lived in a sod hut for thirty more years
until the world dissolved in an ocean of grass.

Think of her sometimes when you pace the earth,
our mother, where she was laid to rest.
The ground was holy, but the wind was harsh
for those who drowned in an ocean of grass.

AFTER THE LAST PRACTICE
(Grinnell, Iowa, November, 1971)

267

Someone said, I remember the first hard crack
Of shoulderpads on the sidelines before a game,
And the bruises that blossom on your arms afterward.

Someone else remembered the faint, medicinal smell
Seeping through the locker room on Saturday mornings,
Getting your ankles taped while a halfback

Frets in the whirlpool about his hamstrings:
Steam on three mirrors, the nervous hiss
Of the first hot shower of the morning.

We talked about the tension mounting all day
Until it became the sound of spikes clattering
Across the locker-room floor, the low banter

Of the last players pulling on their jerseys,
Our middle-linebacker humming to himself
And hammering a forearm against the lockers

While an assistant coach diagrammed a punt
Return for the umpteenth time on his clipboard
For two cornerbacks looking on in boredom...

Eventually, it always came down to a few words
From the head coach–quiet, focused, intense–
While a huge pit opened up in your stomach

268

And the steady buzz of a crowd in the distance
Turned into a minor roaring in your skull
As the team exploded onto the field.

The jitters never disappeared until the opening
Kickoff, the first contact, until a body
Hurtled down the field in a fury

And threw itself against your body
While everything else in the world faded
Before the crunching action of a play, unfolding...

I remember how, as we talked, the flat Midwestern
Fields stretched away into nowhere and nothing,
How the dark sky clouded over like a dome

Covering a chilly afternoon in late November
On the prairie, the scent of pinecones
And crisp leaves burning in the air,

The smoky glow of faces around a small fire.
Someone spoke of road trips and bridge games
In the back of a bus rolling across the plains,

The wooden fenceposts ticking off miles
And miles of empty cornfields and shortgrasses,
Windmills treading their arms, as if underwater,

The first orange lights rising on the horizon—
Jesus, someone said, I never thought it would end
Like this, without pads, without hitting anybody.

But then someone mentioned stepping out of bounds   **269**
And getting blindsided by a bone-wrenching tackle;
Someone else remembered writhing in a pile

Of players coming down on his twisted body.
Torn ligaments. Sprained wrist. A black coin
Blooming under your left eye on Sunday morning.

After all those years of drills and double practices,
Seasons of calisthenics, weightrooms, coaches
Barking orders–missed blocks, squirming fumbles–;

After all those summers of trying to perfect
A sideline pass and a buttonhook, a fly, a flag,
A deep post, a quick pass over the middle;

After the broken patterns and failed double teams,
The July nights sprinting up the stadium stairs
And the August days banging against each other's bodies,

The slow walks home alone in the dusky light–;
After all those injury-prone autumns, not
One of us could explain why he had done it.

What use now is the language of traps
And draws, of power sweeps and desperate on-side
Kicks, of screen passes, double reverses?

But still there was the memory of a sharp cut
Into the open and the pigskin spiraling
Into your hands from twenty yards away,

270   The ecstasy of breaking loose from a tackle
         And romping for daylight, for the green
         Promised land of the empty endzone.

         Someone said, I remember running into the field
         And seeing my girlfriend in the stands at midfield—
         Everyone around her was chanting and shouting

         And the adrenalin was coursing through my body;
         I felt as if I would explode with happiness,
         As if I would never falter, or waver, or die…

         Someone else recollected the endless, losing,
         Thirteen-hour drive home after he had bruised
         A collarbone on the last play of the game,

         The whole bus encased in silence, like a glass
         Jar, like the night itself, clarified. Afterward,
         He recalled the wild joy of his first interception…

         The fire sputtered and smoldered, faded out,
         And our voices trembled in the ghostly woodsmoke
         Until it seemed as if we were partly warriors

         And partly boyscouts ringed around the flame,
         Holding our helmets in our arms and trying
         To understand an old appetite for glory,

         Our raging, innocent, violent, American
         Boyhoods, gone now, vanished forever
         Like the victories and the hard losses.

It was late. A deep silence descended   271
As twilight disintegrated in the night air
And the fire glowered down to embers and ashes,

To red bits of nothing. But no one moved. Oh,
We were burning, burning, burning, burning…
And then someone began singing in the darkness.

Irma McClaurin '73

Irma McClaurin has been writing poetry since the age of 8. She has an M.F.A. in English from the University of Massachusetts and has published three books of poetry: *Black Chicago* (1971), *Songs of the Night* (1974), and *Pearl's Song* (1988). Her poetry has appeared in over 16 anthologies and magazines. Describing herself as "a born-again anthropologist," McClaurin completed a Ph.D. in that subject in 1993 and is currently associate professor of anthropology at the University of Florida, where she is coordinator of the Zora Neale Hurston Diaspora Studies Program, editor of *Transforming Anthropology*, and formerly a board member of the Florida Humanities Council and *The Journal of Feminist Studies*.

Irma's work, even at its angriest and most strongly declamatory, has its poignant and reflective side. She commands an abundant palette of feelings, locales, and personal experience, and has been increasingly drawn toward imagistic writing and other more indirect ways of embodying emotion within her poems.

THE POWER OF NAMES   273

I slip my mother's name on like a glove
and wonder if I will become like her
absolutely.
Years number the times I have worn her pain
as a child, as a teenager, as a woman—my second skin—
or screamed her screams
as she sat, silver head bowed
silent
hedging the storm.

Her name, at times, does not fit me.
I take it, turn it over on my tongue—
a key.
Shape my lips around its vowels
hoping to unlock elusive doors,
understand the instincts
my body scientifically follows.
The family named her Pearl,
a first among them;
yet others have owned this name.
They haunt me.
I follow their destiny.

Each year I return home,
a salmon caught in an act of survival.
I search my mother's face
neatly carved in obsidian
and wonder
how much of myself I owe this woman

274
whose name I have swallowed like a worm.
Her inner soul transferred through the eating.

I slip my mother's name on
with wonder
and become like her
absolutely.

TO A GONE ERA
(My College Days–Class of '73)

The eye of this storm is not quiet.
It sees brown frames inside the city
cutting themselves on jagged loves.
Once we sought to change this world with matches.
Striking our visions against straw promises,
we summoned fire gods and burnt jewish stores
built upon our parents' tragedies, dodged bullets
and walked carefully among the ashes
sifting for our childhood friends
and looking for a place called Future.

We rode books and communed with the "others" in their
                    land;
we spoke their blunted language,
hung our anger on coathooks in dusty ivy hallways
becoming a new minstrel tradition: blacks in whiteface,
shadows tapdancing in cornfields.
We collected barbed words, shot them
through poems with poison edges; used wisdom
of kings & malcolms to ignite bonfires, rising
to taunt the overcast sky that divined our destruction.

Now the voices that once strung themselves like pearls
across the city's neck haunt the bruised nights.
Their sorrow sings through cracked tenement walls.

RETURN TO PUNTA GORDA

Here, in the half life
of a sudden rain shower
I listen to the rooster
trumpet the debute of a new day.

Life moves tight and close
on these quiet streets.
Strangers command attention
while neighbors' faces & names
are remembered and catalogued
like familiar roads & cross streets.

Here, in Punta Gorda
a half-ripened moon
blushes behind the dark finger
of a mahogany tree;

Here, in Punta Gorda,
the sheen of your eyes shined like
twin flecks of black coral;

Here, in Punta Gorda,
your fragrance lingers
like the aftertaste
of sea salt.

And, it is here,
to Punta Gorda,
I shall return
someday
to rest in the sanctuary
of your touch–
a gentle seabreeze
to comfort me
in the hollow emptiness of night.

A MOTHER'S DAY BLESSING

Bless the mothers of Back Street, Queen Street,
Main Street, and all the streets that crisscross
the corners of Punta Gorda Town and Toledo District;
Bless the mothers soothing and cuddling their crying
        babies;
Bless the mothers up at 5AM to wash clothes and bake
        bread;
the mothers who don't eat so their children can be full;
Bless the mothers who walk the hot streets and dusty
        roads
in the midday sun to sell tamales, bread, & tarts;
Bless the mothers who keep watch from dusk to dawn,
without sleep, when their child has fever;

To you, the Village women twisting straw into baskets
for a few dollars so your children's lives will be easier;
To you, the courageous women who take the last
        shilling and pay school fees;
To you, the learned women who speak Garifuna,
        Mayan, Ketchi
the languages of the ancestors so they will not be
        forgotten;
To you, the dancing women whose feet teach us
the rhythms of joy, happiness, & forgetfulness from
        life's troubles;
To you, the drying women who mourn babies, youths
        & husbands
dead from malnutrition, diseases, alcohol, drugs and
        bad luck;

To you, the praying women who only have God to   **279**
    comfort you in hard times;
To you, the hopeful women who dream of a better life
    for your daughters;
To you, women all, mothers all
in Punta Gorda, in Toledo District,
In Belize, Central America;
To you, women and mothers everywhere:

We say thank you.
With every breath we take,
with every pleasure or pain that we feel,
We say thank you for giving birth to us
for guiding us throughout the years
with love and generosity.

We say Bless You.

CHILDHOOD MEMORIES

I

easter morn
i rose
took the rag curlers out
and strutted to church
in pastel
winnie-the-pooh specials
from Sears
and listened to the preacher
talk about
the fair savior.

monday morn
i died again:
nappy hair,
hand-me-down dress
and a mirror
reflecting
no kinship
to Jesus.

II

my flag flew high
on the 4th.
barbecue smells
drifted about.
i even forgot
the little white girl
who spat on me
the day before.

III

i thanked the lord
for no daddy
no shoes
no new dress
two baby brothers
and a turkey.

IV

christmas i watched
mama take
tomorrow's bean money
to buy us
a tree.

282   ADIEU POEM
(In Memory of Duane Casey Taylor '73)

Fragments
sweep over me;
these memories thunder
like spring storms,
sudden, fresh,
frightening even in their intensity.
I glimpse koala bears,
savor musky fragrances of faded bouquets.
And there is even your laughter–
a cacophony–
that echoes beyond the moment past.

This is grief–
a desolate island
where memories flicker
just beyond the escarpment of reality,
so many sweet mirages.
And we sit
in this desert of anguish
awashed with sorrow
redeemed only by moments
with you
captured
somewhere in the past.

Christianne Balk '74   283

A native of upstate New York, Christianne Balk
majored in biology at Grinnell College, where she was
already writing fine poetry. A practiced eye for the
natural world and an ear for bold and shapely language
have drawn high praise and widespread critical atten-
tion in such places as the *New York Times Book Review*,
the *Michigan Quarterly Review*, and the *Virginia
Quarterly Review*. Her collection of poems, *Bindweed*
(Macmillan, 1986), won the 1985 Walt Whitman
award given by the Academy of American Poets to the
best first book of poems in that year. Christianne's
second volume, *Desiring Flight* (Purdue University
Press, 1995), was winner of the Verna Emery Poetry
Prize. Her poems have appeared in *The New Yorker*,
Harpers Magazine, the *New Republic*, *Ploughshares*,
Poetry Northwest, and many other places.

  After Grinnell, with a trained biologist's view of
things still very much part of her equipment,
Christianne entered the University of Iowa Writers'
Workshop where she earned an M.F.A. in poetry. She
has taught at the University of Alaska-Fairbanks, the
Port Townsend Writing Conference, and the University
of Washington Distance Learning Program. So many
strong poems based upon her life in Alaska add up to a
good case for considering Christianne Balk that region's
unofficial poet laureate. But for all her detailed and
uncanny responsiveness to wild places and things, these
images inhabit and animate rather than overwhelm her

284   imaginative understanding of human courage, sorrow, attachment, and longing.

   She now lives in Seattle with her husband and daughter.

ELEGY   **285**

In Wainwright they say the plane went down in the
    Brooks Range, perhaps near Porcupine River, or
    perhaps in the Arctic Ocean;
It was spring, the rivers were breaking up, and the mist
    settled in for weeks.
The plane went down in March, when it rains one day
    and snows the next;
When the ice fields split into islands big enough to
    crush ships.
The plane went down in the early spring, when the
    snow still drifts in the wind, snow so fine it works
    into the tightest weave of a man's coat;
In the north, where the snow is hardened and serrated
    by winter winds, where metal sled runners wear
    out in days, and where men do not leave heel
    marks;
In the spring, when the winds begin to drop, when the
    snow turns soft and honeycombed, and cannot
    support a man's weight;
In the spring, when the winds leave, and the insects
    come, swarms of insects that can weaken a man
    until he cannot walk;
In the far north, where magnetic compasses are useless.
Snowshoe frames can be made of metal from plane
    keels, sleds built from wings, harnesses woven from
    shroud lines;
Cloudy streams of fresh water can be found; and
    salmon, tomcod, needlefish, and pike caught;

286   But the Brooks Range stretches from Cape Lisburne to
            Demarcation Point, and few of its mountains are
            mapped.
       The plane went down in the north, where valley
            glaciers crack into crevasses above deep, granite
            beds;
       In the spring, when rivers swell with melt water, when
            snowbridges are swept away, and debris dams up
            the streams;
       In the north, where the overflow fills the flatland with
            shallow, swampy lakes.
       Beaver, marmot, and ground squirrel can be trapped;
            and molting spruce grouse, arctic loon, and
            ptarmigan can be snared.
       Bushes can be dug for the starchy roots; cup-fungus,
            bracken, and the inner white bark of willow,
            poplar, and birch can be eaten;
       But the north is filled with rose-capped mushroom,
            water hemlock, baneberry, and amanita.
       A plane crashed six years ago in the Bering Sea, in water
            so cold it paralyzed the pilot's hands, but he used
            his teeth to lash himself to a raft with ripcord.
       A man went under for forty minutes in the Yukon
            River, but was pulled up breathing because the
            water had been just cold enough.
       But masses of sea-ice crowd into the bays in the spring,
            colliding with each other and the coast, and the
            booming can be heard for miles.
       A woman lifted an ice-wall in Kotzebue, fracturing her
            spine, but she held the ice up so her husband could
            crawl out.

A plane crashed near Eagle, and a woman dragged her
   husband from the fuselage, and she melted snow in
   her mouth, and brought it to him, until help came.
A Galena trapper was lost two years ago, but his wife
   waited, and pounded beef suet, berries, and bacon
   with a wooden mallet into pemmican, for his next
   trip out, and he was found;
But tundra streams wander aimlessly in the spring, and
   often lead to marshes filled with mosquitoes,
   midges, and blackflies.

288

LEAVING SAND COUNTY:
APRIL 21, 1948
(Aldo Leopold died on this day
while fighting a grass fire.)

Under the roughleg
hawk who hovers like a smooth-
feathered bomb waiting

to drop on the marsh,
bare dogwood stems stand exposed
against the hill. I

see men run back and
forth, trying to fight the grass
fire–burning, burning.

Snipe winnow, coots cluck,
white pinions beat the water.
The geese are leaving.

If only I could
stand up now like the others.
Something pulls me up,

flies me north, drops me
above cold, spring-fed streams hemmed-
in by alder. I

pay out more line. Cast
out as the wind swirls the stream,
shaking like a brown

miller. I wade waist
deep through the green cave of tree
branches and the white

throat rolls lazily
in the dark pool as he sucks
feathers down his throat.

The line straightens. I
ease him upstream around each
bend in the river,

slowly, as if I
were the current. I gently
pull him in. Twisting,

as if still swimming,
the trout twists in the wet alder
leaves lining my creel.

If only I could
stay. Here, where only woodcocks
spiral down like stalled

planes. Here, where burn marks
in the grass are covered by
the wide-sweeping arc

of an owl's wings.

OLD MINTO

Night never comes. Dawn elbows
morning in, shrugs off dusk. I think

of river people hunched in flat-
bottomed boats, tree-anchored, waiting

for the river to recede. Rain rots
timber frames. Snowmelt sags the ceilings. Cabins
slide off poled spruce stilts. I stir

the smudge fire bare-handed, step

into the smoke. Yellow anemones
smolder. The blackflies hum,
carry bits of me away.
Aspens twist, bent by fire. Where are

the flames? Eggs, berries, and roots lie

drenched. Fish baskets tangle
in their own lines. Dip nets float

aimlessly. Pike escape downstream.

Moose wade garnished with flag iris stems
easy in the village green, and slip

unstartled into shadows spun from balsam   **291**
poplar to cinquefoil. Leather lashings
come undone. The hands that braided everything

are gone. Old laps rest on the ridge.
Heavy ground, tilled by frost, barely

holds the picket fence stamped with stars
and crosses. From up here, the Minto Flats
stretch as far as I can see

each lake, creek, rill, mire, pond, and bog

named by people whose words
burr like the wings of swans returning

to nest
in the spring, in the rain, in the sun, in the wind, in the sloughs'

exaltations of mosquitoes.

DEAR HIPPOPOTAMUS

Move over, you tiny-eared, boulder-bodied
hog, let me kneel down with you, bleary-eyed
and mud-sunk. Water horse! Let me wallow
in your ivory-stained, peg-toothed dreams, following
the cool, sun-chased shadows while flamingos
arrive screeching pink from their distant coasts.
News of shocking continents! Let's listen
to the twirling, sliding, feathered whistles
of their courting colors, blurred and whirlpooled
down still air, like the bristling pods of burr seeds,
or the spinning of the wasp-stung beetle,
or the circling of the zinc-lined stars, reeling
night after night above your small, revolving
ears, while our great, slow, rock-bound bodies sleep.

TONGA RIDGE

Sitting on the slope
scattered with ponchos, diapers, spare socks,
and the caterpillar-brown army blanket

the quiet inhalations of Elizabeth's sleep
blending with the bustle of leaves and plastic bags,
her father and grandmother talking
softly, picking berries

the swish of my hand
sweeping the mosquitoes from her face,
the flies and the bees muttering,

and far beyond the dark green forests
slashed with the silver dead,
something drones like a slow-moving Cessna,
though there are no planes in sight.

For a moment I see
beyond the snow patches and the distant
jagged ridges
veined with gravel run-offs too steep to hold trees

how many times this trail has been traveled
by one family or another,
led by the eldest woman

who knows the way up the Foss River road
to the trail head,

294
one woman leading one small group single file
into the pale green pines,

through the long-bristled branches draped
with moss, and the new platinum-gray needles billowing

along the ridge
where layers of warm air trapped
by the high, flamboyant storm clouds
are streaked with cool breezes

and into the thistle-gone-to-seed meadows
and the fireweed hung with mauve stork-bill pods,

to a spot where a mother might rest
with her child sleeping at her side,
on the blanket pressing the wild grass
close in with the blueberries' maroon-edged leaves
and the triangular handshakes of ferns.

THE WILD DOG'S STEPS

Envy the wild dog stalking on the snow's
    wavering path and his ice-imprinted steps.
        The water snake disappears. Her rope-looped
wake takes longer to erase, diminishing
    in ever-widening arcs. Falling always
        down, the rain is pulled towards the earth's iron
heart. A pair of hawks press their bellies, turn hooked heads,
    entangle talons, free-fall toward slate
        roofs. Sprung at the seam, each barely touching,
the Scot's Broom's pods burst open, twisting old
    husks in two. Swooping north over the slope
        in broad day, the short-eared owl embraces
the hill beyond the chain-link fence with the wide

    ovals of her flight. Hooped wings direct the air.
        Dark lines ellipse shoulders, face. Overhead,
the geese hurl their collective weight along
    triangulated necks. Does the milkweed
        doubt the wind? Held out like children's hands,
the hawthorne's leaves cup themselves,
    fastened to green limbs shooting up and down
        in a rush of yellow-red as bent as
water falling from a spring no one can
    see. A pheasant whirs her blustered feathers
        upwards. Another nests his ring-marked chest
in sable grass, parting wide with wasps. Yet
    somehow each is whole. Dear pale, displaced feet,
        abandoned! Envy them.

296   *Brad Clompus '74*

After Grinnell, Brad Clompus earned a master of fine arts degree from the University of Iowa Writers' Workshop and pursued graduate study in English at Tufts University. He lives and works in Medford, Mass., where he is a development consultant to arts organizations. He has been a proposal writer and grants administrator at Harvard, Brown, and Tufts Universities and has directed the grants program at Poets & Writers, a service organization in New York City. At various times, he has taught composition and literature at Tufts University, Baruch College, Polytechnic University, and Bentley College.

Brad's poetry and essays have appeared in such periodicals as *Tampa Review*, *Passages North*, *West Branch*, *Cream City Review*, *Poet Lore*, and *Blueline*. He is editor of *The Mystic River Review*, an online literary journal, and since 1996 has taught poetry workshops at the Arlington (Massachusetts) Center for the Arts. He cites as key influences Donald Justice, Galway Kinnell, Robert Bly, Philip Levine, and Elizabeth Bishop.

A typical poem by Brad Clompus offers a sharply etched account of a particular experience, closely observed but rhetorically uninflated: watching a moose swim to its death, exploring a cave, paddling a canoe on a Maine pond. It is poetry that scrupulously refuses to give you more than you need. Little ingratiating gab; no emotional posturing; fresh images without cute touches; not a word of tender sentiment or good advice.

CAMAC BATHHOUSE

Door in a sooty brick wall
off a cobbled alley. My father opens it.
We go steeply down. Another door.
A shrivelled counter man takes our wallets and keys,
stows them in a black box.
From below, a musk of camphor and pine.
Down more stairs, tiled walls,
heat rising as we near the linen room,
tended by men in sleeveless t-shirts.
We take two hot sheets, wrap diagonally,
shoulder to waist. My father tucks mine in.
Three glass doors, fogged on the inside:
Pine, Spruce, Desert.
In the Desert, ten men on a slatted bench—
a few thin and pale as salamanders;
some obese, black hair whorling on chest and paunch.
We slump in the heat, side by side.
A man enters with a tray of glasses;
we signal lazily, are served.
Don't drink too fast, my father warns.
I nuzzle the glass, sip cool air that floats
in a globe of vapor above the ice.
When we're cooked, we go to the pool, its low ceiling
webbed by membranes of light, aqua and yellow.
We dive in nude. I, the newly whelped seal, and he,
the great sea-turtle, blurry underwater, arms swooping,
hair slicked straight back, bubbles erupting from his nose.
I climb out and watch from the ledge,
my limbs folded, sleek and dry.

298 In the weight room, he hugs a long leather bag
hung by a chain, while I whump into it,
left hook, left hook, straight right.
Braced against the mat by his heels,
he says how hard I hit, that I'm some tiger.
When I tire, he goes to the speed-bag,
holds the bag still with one hand and peers at it.
Jabs, assesses, waits a few beats,
then resumes, picks up speed, his fists
circling like twin oblique gears, never touching,
inscribing arcs, metronomic. Right then,
I know that I will never punch like that.
Then we talk about the schoolyard bully.
His advice: *Tell him he has a yellow stripe*
running down his back.
So I practice that phrase, precisely.
Two weeks later, on a weedy lot behind a gas station,
I take the kid on. A little crowd surrounds us,
urges the first punch. We slap and poke,
tear each other's shirts, until disheartened, we give in.
No one can say who wins.
Nobody really wins that fight.

Our last stop underground:
the Sun Room—a box of burnished metal
like a midnight diner, or a train car
before it becomes a train.
We put on smoke-lensed goggles,
walk in, breathe the scorched, sterile air,
stand side by side
with a half dozen naked men.

No introductions; we do not talk.
We do not look
at the ultraviolet tubes
lining the box.
We just stand there in a line
and take it,
watch our reflected skin
as it darkens.

THE FAR SIGNALS

On the floor, three a.m.,
an inch from my ear,
El Paso, Omaha, Grand Forks.
It's not song that I want,
but talk. Say anything;
sell me anything. What
were your highs and lows,
Sioux Falls? When is
the Ogallala Boosters Club
meeting, and where? Who's
the best Chevrolet dealer
in the whole Delaware valley?
I rarely get more
than half an answer,
before it fades, then migrates.
Denver wants to be Dayton.
Boston wants to be Abilene.
But as I turn
from station to station,
I hear of miracles.
They sell the identical burger
from Gary to Huntsville.
And the President, lopped
from his syllable in Pittsburgh,
flies through the static,
lands in Sacramento,
rejoins the word.

I heard the first act
of the Mystery Theatre
twice between Topeka and Toledo.
About a statue of Venus,
and a man who put his ring
on her finger, as a joke.
For Venus, it was no joke.
She was much in love.
He begged her for release,
but she also begged,
pitifully, inside his dreams.
He still refused.
I don't know what happened to them,
or in which city.
I changed, wanting the news.
I heard of a panic
somewhere, which made gold
blast heavenward.
And a regime balancing
on the scarp of oblivion.
A melancholy leader, faintly
from the capital, pleading
for his sore nation.
This was near sign-off.
The station identified itself
with four cryptic letters.
And soon the rest
announced theirs,
one after another,
the letters aglow like neon,
hung free in the moonless night.

SPELUNK

From prairie in the light,
elevator down fifty floors,
carrying a miner's lamp and knee pads.
At bottom, the door opens
to rough walls, limestone,
glazed with silver pin-pricks.
The guide, clean-cut in olive drabs—
too young, I think, for the underworld.
She kneels on the ground, lays
silky red strips on the floor, says
this will bring us back.
We hunch over, enter a
sloping black shaft.
Our lamps make cones
where we turn our heads;
outside the arcs, night
is unredeemed. The ceiling clamps.
Half upright, almost crawling,
midway down evolution,
my head cracks into something
sharp, uncompromising.
I live to speak of it.
The tunnel turrets, deadends
in a gallery with three holes.
Choices. The guide offers
me tape, but do I want to choose?
She and the others disappear, feet
splayed, their last parts to vanish.
I choose one and belly in.

A clenched tract; the walls, ragged,
shear thin strips from my clothes.
Elemental splinters down my shirt.
Breathing, through teeth, fine mineral dust.
I shouldn't be here. It narrows;
the earth cramps more.
Almost a flounder, I wriggle,
spine along. Finally, the fissure
relents. Hands first, then head,
I flop into an oval chamber.
Shake grit off my hands, look around.
A hole in the ceiling.
One hour left to do as I will;
I could go up there…

Before she disappeared,
the girl, in a husky voice,
too old for her, maybe,
in love with the place she had led us,
had offered this advice:
Stop somewhere.
Turn off your light,
Try to be still.
I flick it off. A swarm
of whirling sparks fade
to dense purple, stain
to swollen black.
The quiet pushes softly,
deftly raises pressure.
In my ears, a high pure whine,
the body's white noise, or

304

signals from somewhere else.
I am resting on the submarine
after the depth-charge has hit.
And I am glad to be done.
No panic, no shouting
allowed here. I am alone
with my flooded heart,
and the walls are drawing in
slowly, sweetly, with great tenderness.

TRAILING IT HOME

Expelled from the woods at noon,
bark-brown, reeking of swamp,
with tender, palmate antlers
weightless over his bulk,
he clopped down
the town's main street,
his eyes fogged and serene
like a martyr's.
When they spotted him,
pointed and yelled,
he began to lope. He knew
the way to a stream
which divided the town,
where he slid down the banks,
and plunged to his chest.
The stream left town, flowed
between moss-padded hills
and flushed him to sea.
He swam out with wild
rocking bursts of will, striding
invisibly, his paradise
just beyond the dusky swells.
Pushing a translucent billow,
a party in a skiff chased,
caught up, prodded with oars,
tried to force him back.
They saw wet, felty antlers,
a cone of snout,
and behind, a hump

like coconut-husk.
He couldn't be diverted.
He had something great in mind,
before he tired, gasped,
blew like a whale,
then drowned.
They roped his hind quarters
so he wouldn't sink.
On the dock, he weighed in
at six seventy-two. Five families
feasted that week.
All of this is on record.
The next day's paper
had four pictures on page one
of the moose's progress:
at the edge of the woods,
trotting down the street,
wading in the stream,
being dragged back.
In this last one,
his long brown head
blurs into the tunnel
of its wake.

VIEW OF MT. KATAHDIN
FROM FROST POND

The canoe stalls
when the paddles lift, pivots,
a needle seeking north,
swings in the finger tides
nudging us from muddy springs.
We drift to center. Spiralled
over moss-felted woods
that circle the pond,
washes of yellowed blue
on verge of lapis, hints
of onyx at the core, space
bottomless above us.
We paddle a bit, just to
sense we move. Only from here,
this precise wavering point
of the trembling pond, does
Katahdin appear: rumpled
flanks of the peak, its hard husk
torn by slides, scarred and patched,
but bold-stroked, sharp-shouldered.
From this range, details
of the quick or the dead
withheld, the slope's doors
clamped, bronze-brown
in the receding light.
We hold the paddles still,
to stay, not stray from it,
until the peak is snuffed.
Then we point the canoe

308

towards where we started,
the water beneath us
dark, smooth,
thinned molasses.
First stars; risen coin of moon.
We skim slowly, watch
for subtle snags and rocks,
keep silent for loons,
their undulant hoooos
homing to parts we don't visit.
We're sleek in the water,
as if drawn by strings;
the paddles slide in, spawn
whirlpools, and we slip forward.
Though I'm a strong swimmer,
and we skirt the shore, I'm afraid
on this cone of dark.
You want to linger, wait for stars
to burn holes through the night,
for the moon's mercuric haze.
But we go–the paddles slosh,
drip as they rise, our wake
a confluence of small streams.
Awkward, when finally we bump
into the dock–two dull strokes
on a drum. My heart
beats fast. We look back
but at the wrong time,
from an imprecise place.
Still it is there, regardless
of what we think,
blacking a wedge of sky.

WOMAN BATHING IN THE WEST RIVER   **309**

Emerged from a green-needled wall,
fabric of woods risen as sheer terrace,
the woman and dog settle on a large flat rock–
her black shepherd, not far from wolf,
wades in, lifts a dripping paw,
freezes in place, peers through panes of stream,
then looks back at her, pleadingly,
and she, aloof from all the swimmers,
hair curtained long around her oval face,
slides her long legs into the glimmer.
Where she steps the soft tadpoles scatter,
then slowly settle to rest,
so heavy this time of year they do not
wish to move, gravid with
change that is coming, their sharp little tails
withering away, futile as afterthoughts.

David Mura '74

Poet, writer of nonfiction, critic, playwright, performance artist, lecturer–David Mura's is among the most urgent and widely-gifted Asian American voices speaking today. The blight of racism stirs pained personal and familial memories and is the object of his searing indignation; it also moves him toward the furthest, often unexpected, reaches of human sympathy.

David Mura's poems have appeared in many journals including *The New Republic, The America Poetry Review, The Nation, The New England Review,* and *Crazyhorse.* He is the author of numerous essays about race and multiculturalism for such publications as *Mother Jones, The New York Times, The Utne Reader,* and *The Graywolf Annual V: Multi-Cultural Literacy.* His criticism has appeared in *The Boston Review, The Hungry Mind Review,* and elsewhere. A book of critical essays, tentatively titled *Notes for a New Century,* is scheduled for publication in the University of Michigan Press Poets on Poetry series.

David's first book of poems, *After We Lost Our Way,* won the 1989 National Poetry Series Contest. His second, *The Colors of Desire* (1995), won the Carl Sandburg Literary Award from the Friends of the Chicago Public Library. His two much-acclaimed memoirs are *Turning Japanese: Memoirs of a Sensei,* which won a 1991 Josephine Miles Book Award from the Oakland PEN and was listed in the *New York Times* Notable Books of the Year, and *Where the Body Meets*

Memory: An Odyssey of Race, Sexuality, and Identity
(1996). Film adaptations of his work have been
broadcast on public television, and he has been featured
in the Bill Moyers PBS series, *The Language of Life*.

The performance piece *Secret Colors*, a collabora-
tion with the African American writer Alexs Pate,
premiered at the Walker Art Center, Minneapolis, in
1995. David has taught at the University of Minnesota,
St. Olaf College, The Loft, and the University of
Oregon; he gives readings and speaks on the issue of
race and multiculturalism throughout the country.
David makes his home in Minneapolis with his wife,
Dr. Susan Sencer '76, and their three children.

David Mura's recollections of the part Grinnell
played in arousing and nurturing his interest in writing
are generous and vivid: "The appearances at Grinnell of
poets Donald Hall, Denise Levertov, Donald Justice,
and Christopher Middleton were important," he says.
"My 'Major British Poets' course with Professor
Connelly where we did imitations of Spenser and Pope
was, in a way, my poetic beginning. It led to the poetry
workshop I did with Professor Cavanagh–I think a first
on campus–and an independent project with Professor
Cleaver on modern poetry. Cleaver was notorious for
allowing students to move beyond the prescribed
curriculum, and I feel grateful for the chance he took
with me."

from
LETTERS FROM TULE LAKE
INTERNMENT CAMP (1942–45)

Dear Michiko,

Do songs sound different in prison?
I think there are more spaces between the words.
I think, when the song ends, the silence
does not stop singing. I think
there is nothing but song.

Matsuo's back, his bruises almost healed,
a tooth missing. His *biwa*
comes out again with the stars, a nightly
matter. He sends his regards.

Do you get fed these putrid grey beans?
I hope you haven't swallowed too
many of them. They put my stomach
in a permanent revolt, shouting no emperor
would ever feed his people so harshly.
I agree. Let's you and I grow
skinny together. Let's keep the peace.

Any second the lights will go off.

I look around me and see many
honest men who hide their beauty
as best they can.

I think that's what the whites hate,
our beauty, the way we carry the land
and the life of plants inside us,
seedlings and fruit, the flowers
and the flush tree, fields freed of weeds.

Why can't they see the door's inside them?
If someone found an answer to that,
they'd find an answer to why
those who are hungry and cold
go off to battle to become hungrier
and colder, farther from home.

Nine o'clock. The lights all out.

*

…Sometimes, Michiko,
I think of my greenhouse,
how I used to stand at night in its fleshy,
steaming dark and say, "These are the most
beautiful orchids and roses in the world."
And their fragrance seeped inside me,
stayed even when I sold them.

What is it like now in Tokyo?
They say it has
sunk like a great ship.

Forgive me. Blessed
with a chance to talk to my wife,

314

more beautiful than any greenhouse rose,
all I can do is moan.
And yet, if I didn't tell you,
I would be angry at you for not listening,
blaming you for what I haven't spoken.

And it's too late for that...

When you write back, please
tell me what country I'm in.

I feel so poor now.
These words are all I own.

GRANDFATHER-IN-LAW

It's nothing really, and really, it could have been worse,
and of course, he's now several years dead, and his
widow, well, if oftentimes she's somewhat distracted,
overly cautious when we visit—after all, Boston isn't
New York—she seems, for some reason, enormously
proud that there's
              now a writer in the family,
and periodically, sends me clippings about the poet
laureate, Thoreau, Anne Sexton's daughter,
              Lowell, New England literary lore—
in which I fit, if I fit at all, simply because I write in
English—as if color of skin didn't matter
              anymore.
Still, years ago, during my first visit to Boston, when we
were all asleep, he, who used to require that my wife
memorize lines of Longfellow or Poe and recite them on
              the phone,
so that, every time he called, she ran outdoors and had
to be coaxed back, sometimes with
              threats, to talk to Pops
(though she remembers too his sly imitations of Lincoln,
ice cream at Brighams, burgers
              and fries, all the usual grandfatherly treats),
he, who for some reason was prejudiced against Alba-
nians—where on earth did he find them I
              wondered—
who, in the thirties, would vanish to New York, catch a
show, buy a suit, while up north, the gas and water bills

316

pounded the front door (his spendthrift ways startled
me with my
grandfather's resemblance),
who for over forty years came down each morning,
"How's the old goat?" with a tie only his
wife could knot circling his neck,
he slipped into my wife's room—we were unmarried at
the time—and whispered so softly she thought he almost
believed she was really asleep, and was saying this like a
wish or spell, some bohunk
miscalculated Boston sense of duty:
"Don't make a mistake with your life, Susie. Don't make
a mistake…" Well. The thing that gets me now, despite
the dangling rantings I've let go, is that, at least at
that time,
he was right: There was, inside me, some pressing, raw
unpeeled persistence, some libidinous
desire for dominance
that, in the scribbled first-drafts of my life, seemed to
mark me as wastrel and rageful,
bound to be unfaithful,
to destroy, in some powerful, nuclear need, fissioned
both by childhood and racism,
whatever came near—
And I can't help but feel, forgiving him now, that if she
had listened, if she had been awake, if this flourishing
solace, this muscled-for happiness, shared by us now, had
never awakened, he would have become for me a symbol
of my rage and self-destruction, another raw, never
healing wound,

and not this silenced grandfatherly presence, a crank
and scoundrel, red-necked Yankee who created
      the delicate seed of my wife, my child.

IN AMERICA

The season of searing Santa Annas,
brush fires that flare all night in the hills, taut
vibrant emanations of light, *ojiisan*

would drive them to the Pacific, just before
sundown and the long steaming L.A. night.
In that silver Packard reeking of cigar,

the children laughed and shouted, sang with him,
never understanding the words, China
nights, a soldier somewhere in Asia, swimming

in his solitude, the girl from home. Soon
he shuttled them out beneath the night sky,
and he talked on the beach of his boyhood

in Shingu, his father, going back to Japan
for *omiyai*, their mother. Told them again
they'd been born here, this was their homeland,

but someday he'd go back to die, rich as an emperor.
Nonsense, says his wife, as they clamber back,
and he opens the door like a chauffeur,

tipping his cap. The children giggle. And none
of them knows this life is condemned,
even as they fall asleep to his humming,

syllables that flash and vanish in their dreams
years later in Chicago, Stamford, Miami,
cities of their small diaspora. They wake, groping,

to find the song vanished, a faint wind searing
their faces, still scented with sea, cigar smoke,
this sadness they cannot name. And each hears

only the breathing of a companion, blue
shadows of morning betraying a normalcy
none of them imagines, sleeping in the back

of a Packard in 1930, '36 or '40.
These are the years of expectation, elation,
when he is unbroken, she not yet dreaming,

as in the fall of '41, of flames soaring,
exploding off the sea, some divine wind
raining damnation, disintegration, war.

Years in America when my father was a boy.
When my father was a Jap. In America.

WORDS ON MY TONGUE
for Li-Young Lee

I am nine, sitting in a circle with our teacher.
I am to read out loud. Though I know these words
–*ball, the, I, throw, boy, girl*–they lodge
in my throat, dry as cotton balls, a cough that won't leave.
My teacher wears a look of concern or impatience,
it doesn't matter. My classmates giggle or shift
in boredom, it doesn't matter. The words
lie like ammunition on the page. I will not fire them.
(The gun aims at the center of my chest.)
The minutes pass, the day is long. Finally,
the teacher asks the next student to read on.

Deep at night, that first winter,
I lay in the cupola
of my sheets and rubbed
my hands together, half
in prayer, half
like two sticks, praying for fire.
Like those who took us in
as sponsors on Sunday,
I was asking for the Holy Spirit
to enter me, to speak in tongues of flame.

We were Chinese, from Sadec, just outside Saigon.
There the river flooded through the delta,
a miracle of mud and substances abounding
in the current–crates, chairs, water buffalo, branches
and sometimes bodies, the drowned
ones, eyes turned toward some other world.

My brother almost drowned there once.
My mother slapped me for taking him down.
That sting still rings in my ear like a gong.

I knew I spoke with this accent.
It was visible as a hump
or the limp my sister walks with,
the metal braces that reverberate her steps.
The noise that emptied from my mouth
contained a color I could not eradicate,
a grating sing song
like horsehair of a violin, a Chinese violin,
and even as I opened my mouth
I could see, in the eyes of a listener,
if they were white, spreading in every direction
across their face, a judgment
as inevitable as at evening
comes the descending night.

Uncomely noise, ugly noise, ching-chong
Chinamen noise, cavity ridden
and sounding of brown gums, yellowed teeth,
contorted lips struggling like some ape to speak,
and unlike the splinter
father drew with delicacy from my palm,
removing a pain I'd lived with all day,
down the streets of the city, the graffiti and traffic,
there was nothing he could do,
nor my mother. The words sat
on my tongue, like the questions
that sat inside my ear—*What did you say? What did he say?*

322

And yet,
even then, I was moving away,
coming to the time
when I would stand with father, mother,
before my teacher
and translate to them
both the praise, which I embellished,
and the checks, which I altered, fights
on the asphalt schoolyard of broken glass
and a rumbling in my stomach
that spoke incessantly of fear.
Deep in the magical jungle,
in some country we traveled
to, my parents were wandering,
and I had to lead them, word by word,
in the grocer's, before the lawyer, my teacher,
to meaning, sweet land of comprehension
rising like an island from the chaos of oceans
back in the beginning when God made the word and the world.

You children, you who take your foreign parents
into these unfamiliar streets
know this trembling, this fear;
and even though you speak *for* them,
you cannot speak your fear.

So what is it I do now in the corporation?
I open my eyes to numbers, their possible blossoming,
beauty comprehensible to my tongue,
and only those occasional afternoons,
speaking under fluorescence,

like a prisoner confessing sins of the previous regime,

does it come back in the faces before me–

The smirk in their smiles, the sliver on my tongue.

And I know then
I have bitten
a ceiling of glass
which will never shatter
with the words I speak to you now
so like the words I spoke as a child

once upon a time, long ago: *Boy, ball, throw, me.*

THE YOUNG ASIAN WOMEN

The young Asian women are shaving their heads,
piercing eyelids and ears. They stare holes
in curators, shop clerks and geisha chasers,
bubble gum popping like caps in their jaws.
Their names? Juliana, Vong, Lee and Lily.
Could be Mina from the outskirts of Tokyo
but more likely she's Nkauj'lis of the famous
or infamous Lyfongs (depending on your clan
and your anti-Communist persuasions).
Check out that siren named Sonia too in love
with her looks, a nasty curl of Seoul
in her smile. Or if her name is Hoa,
she's tough as her mother, bad girl, bitch,
it doesn't matter, she'll survive like nettles,
flower in what ditch she finds herself, with
or without a man, or her lesbian lover who left
for Alaska, the smell of bearshit on the trail.
With her Taiwanese aunt, digs tales of Toisan
ladies, dragons and the water marsh where bandit
ghosts steal years with a kiss, talking tongues
down your throat to your belly, slipping
a demon seed inside you to grow. Oh, they
are like that, these young women, their art alive
like pepper on your tongue, hurtling hurt
with a half pint gleaming on the nightstand;
they know how mysteriously the body is written,
how thundering colors of Benneton befit
statistics on garment workers in the Third
and First Worlds. They know Woman Warrior,

bell hooks, how the moon waxes red like
the sheets where they write out scripts, stories
and poems, unwrapping their dreams before
you, a palm of paint, pearls, I-Ching stones.
Their boots are black and buckled, their jeans frayed,
their lips bruised purple or incandescent red;
on the dance floor their bodies catch hip-hop
as a sail seizes breeze, turbulent, taut and driven.
Their voices are hoarse after nights on the floor,
their faces smeared with sweat. Their cheeks glow.
They scare the pants off the young men they know.

A WINTER'S TALE

How did I lose and find my life? The stars have their homes,
the moon needs no country,
and the snow
distilling
its icy existence
to a moment on my palm
fears no vanishing
but falls
and falls in its dreaming
and real existence. So
I stand in my yard
staring up at the window
where your face
might appear, calling me
in, bathed in the sweat
of my running mile
after mile up the river
in search of the body that leaves me
no wisdom
but only the soft
flaking and fattening
of a soul past forty.
If I were a young
lover, I would fly
like a sprite
up to that window, scraping
to be let in, calling
your name like a wound
in my side, and only

your touch like a preacher
electrified with the godhead
lightning the believer, fainting
him back to earth, might conjure a salve
to the slashing
you've left me to hold.
But I'm no longer
twenty, I'm only scooping
snow from the walk, not
bleeding in the cold. And that
same sweet light up there
stays me these moments
where your face won't
appear, as you know
already what I'll do
moments from now—
Open the door and walk
as I have half my life
back into yours.

328   *Ray Young Bear '76*

Who and what defines us? What makes us who we are? Who, indeed, are we? Ray Young Bear's work addresses such questions not only as a Native American but for all of us. Ray's writing reflects a deep and knowledgeable consciousness of his Mesquakie heritage, but he is no less a participant in our contemporary society's rapid and uncertain movement away from much that tradition, heritage, and rootedness were once counted on to provide. Authentic and distinct, yet somehow universal, his vision and experience pose a strong challenge to stereotypical and sentimental notions about those Americans who have lived here longest but are known the least.

Ray Young Bear was born and raised in the Mesquakie Tribal Settlement near Tama, Iowa. He attended Grinnell and various other colleges and universities and has taught in the Institute of American Indian Arts at Eastern Washington University, the University of Iowa, and Iowa State University. In 1993 he was awarded an honorary doctorate from Luther College, and in 1997 he received The Ruth Suckow Award for *Remnants of the First Earth*, which was judged that year's outstanding work of fiction about Iowa. To date he has published two books of poetry, *Winter of the Salamander* and *The Invisible Musician*, and two works of fiction. His poems have appeared widely in such places as *American Poetry Review, The Gettysburg Review, The Kenyon Review, New York*

Quarterly, *Northwest Review*, *Tri-Quarterly*, and *Virginia Quarterly Review*. He is currently at work on a third volume of poetry, the last novel in a trilogy, and a book of nonfiction. He and his wife Stella are co-founders of the Woodland Song & Dance Troupe of Arts Midwest.

FROM THE SPOTTED NIGHT

In the blizzard
while chopping wood
the mystical whistler
beckons my attention.
Once there were longhouses
here. A village.
In the abrupt spring floods
swimmers retrieved our belief.
So their spirit remains.
From the spotted night
distant jets transform
into fireflies who float
towards me like incandescent
snowflakes.
The leather shirt
which is suspended
on a wire hanger
above the bed's headboard
is humanless; yet when one
stands outside the house,
the strenuous sounds
of dressers and boxes
being moved can be heard.
We believe someone wears
the shirt and rearranges
the heavy furniture,
although nothing
is actually changed.
Unlike the Plains Indian shirts

which repelled lead bullets,
ricocheting from them
in fiery sparks,
this shirt is the means;
this shirt *is* the bullet.

ALL STAR'S THANKSGIVING

At midnight
when we finally signalled for
and received permission
to go outside and relieve
ourselves, I stepped off
the porch onto a steep cliff.
Immediately, I dropped
to the ground for fear
I would tumble down
the mountainside.
"Get up," said Facepaint,
the trickster who brought
me to his relative's *amanita*
congregation.
"There are no mountains
in the Midwest," he added.
Later, after he got me upright,
we went back inside.
Comforted by people,
I sat back against
the log cabin wall
and closed my watery eyes.
Suddenly, I was sitting on
a tropical beach with my legs
in the vibrant surf. In the breeze
I felt the sun's warmth. I became
sleepy, and when my head sank
into the wall, I woke up.
I soon discovered that

my left leg was missing.
I truly thought I had
sacrificed it as a brake
on the mountainside.

EAGLE CROSSING, JULY 1975

Without Selene
he didn't know what to do.
As was the case with his grandfather,
he felt no recourse but to start
a sculpture-mask,
hollowing out
the dish at first,
and then carving the face
of the Big Footed One,
Me ma ki ka ta ta.
He saw himself
as this reclusive entity,
confined to wait for
the glacier-aided breeze
of a summer night.
There were frequent
dreams that she would soon
return to caress the areas
where his human arms
and legs once were;
her perfumed fingers
would come through
the cottonwood mask
and touch his closed eyes.
To him, the summer was simply
the odor of accidentally burnt
skin, filtering like snake newborn
through the oven racks.
He sat before warm, uneaten
t.v. dinners, and he paid

little heed to self-collapsing
trash bags.

No longer could he
remember the details
of crisp frosted mornings
when he unerringly invited
names of both enemy
and relative into
his offering of flint chips
and shavings from a black
antelope tine. From a silver
Spanish lancepoint, which served
as the body of the feather-fringed
pipe–a symbol of epic campaigns
and Flag Wars–he smoked this mixture
along with Friesland tobacco, and he
thought of the mythical hot sun region
where the-people-who-pulled-up-their-
ladders lived. He saw himself
as a god-like antelope dodging
musket balls before his death.
The crudely-shaped star felt cool
on his chest: Religion & Broken
Hearts, he recited, somewhere
high above the earth's backbone
in the month of Thunder Moon.
Postcard from a suicidal year.

336

Wa ta se Na ka mo ni,
VIET NAM MEMORIAL

Last night when the yellow moon
of November broke through the last line
of turbulent Midwestern clouds,
a lone frog, the same one
who probably announced
the premature spring floods,
attempted to sing.
Veterans' Day, and it was
sore throat weather.
In reality the invisible musician
reminded me of my own doubt.
The knowledge that my grandfathers
were singers as well as composers—
one of whom felt the simple utterance
of a vowel made for the start
of a melody—did not produce
the necessary memory or feeling
to make a *Wa ta se Na ko mo ni,*
Veterans' Song.
All I could think of
was the absence of my name
on a distant black rock.
Without this monument
I felt I would not be here.
For a moment I questioned
why I had to immerse myself
in country, controversy, and guilt;
but I wanted to honor them.

Surely, the song they presently
listened to along with my grandfathers
was the ethereal kind which did not stop.

337

OUR BIRD AEGIS

An immature black eagle walks assuredly
across a prairie meadow. He pauses in mid-step
with one talon over the wet snow to turn
around and see.

Imprinted in the tall grass behind him
are the shadows of his tracks,
claws instead of talons, the kind
that belong to a massive bear.
And he goes by the name:
Me kwi so ta.

And so this aegis looms against the last
spring blizzard. We discover he's concerned
and the white feathers of his spotted hat
flicker, signaling this.

With outstretched wings he tests the sutures.
Even he is subject to physical wounds and human
tragedy, he tells us.

The eyes of the Bear-King radiate through
the thick, falling snow. He meditates the loss
of my younger brother—and by custom
suppresses his emotions.

THE ROCK ISLAND HIKING CLUB

Symbolically, they stand close together
as they have done throughout their lives
on the Black Eagle Child Settlement. They peer
nervously into the canvas-shaded bigtop where
the tribal celebration is about to take place:
Mary Two Red Foot in her brilliant
cotton-white skirt has her one year old,
big-boned grandson, Robert No Body, slung
on her back in a green yarn-fringed shawl.

In the choking humidity, the serrated trim
of the tent vibrates as a concert bass drum
is being tuned. Mary squints in the harsh
daylight and begins talking: *"A kwi ma ka ski
bi ta bi ya ni ni-tte na-ki tta bi wa ki.*
I can't see in there, but they're already
seated." All she can make out are silhouettes
of singers on bales of hay.

Her younger half-sister, Doreen Half Elk,
with unseen hands on hips leans over
and listens intently. In the heat all Doreen
wishes to show is her face. A black and gray-
striped shawl covers her body and head.
Even her feet and shoes are in the dark
shade of her ruffled skirt. She's a statue
whose base is the earth.

340
　　　　　Beside them, sitting in a semi-circle
　　　　　on the ground, four white men in neckties,
　　　　　suspenders, and straw hats are having lunch.
　　　　　The baby, No Body, looks down at the men
　　　　　who are nearly transparent in the hot,
　　　　　July 15, 1932 sun.

Matt Brennan '77   341

Matt Brennan finds that his poetry and his scholarly writing feed into each other. "I pursued a doctorate in English [at the University of Minnesota] rather than the now-conventional M.F.A. because I felt I needed to know more about literature to become a better writer. I chose scholarly projects that complement my creative interests." Since 1985 he has taught literature and creative writing at Indiana State University in Terre Haute, where he is professor of English and has served as director of graduate studies. A very productive scholar, Matt focuses his attention on the English Romantic poets and on the application of Jungian psychology to literature. He is the author of numerous articles and two critical studies: *Wordsworth, Turner and Romantic Landscape: A Study of the Traditions of the Picturesque and the Sublime* (1987) and *The Gothic Psyche: Disintegration and Growth in 19th-Century English Literature* (1997). To date he has also published two books of poetry that bring together poems previously appearing in a variety of journals: *Seeing in the Dark* (1993) and *The Music of Exile* (1994). Currently he is putting together a group of poems based on New Deal artworks.

Described in the *Dictionary of Literary Biography Yearbook* as a "Midwestern poet in the tradition of [James] Wright, Ted Kooser, and Jared Carter," Matt adds to that list of poets he particularly admires and identifies with the names of Sharon Olds, Galway

Kinnell, Seamus Heaney, W.D. Snodgrass, and Mark Strand. Nor does Brennan himself fit a narrowly regional or provincial designation, though his ear for the down-to-earth idiomatic language of middle America is surely one of his important strengths. Others are his refreshingly wide range of interests–revealed even within the familiar bounds of the autobiographical lyric–and a flair for exploring more "objective" modes such as the dramatic monologue.

SIGNS OF LIFE   343

"It took 31 days for former Indiana Gov. Edgar
Whitcomb to sail the Atlantic and even after returning
he's not sure why he made the trip."
          — *Terre Haute Tribune Star*, 3/26/90

Sometimes I close my eyes and I'm still
At sea, catching the cold Atlantic trade winds
That rode the looping hills of gray-green waves
And whipped white spume in my face like aftershave.
My month between the Ghana coast and the Caribbean
I lived another lifetime, was someone else.
Each splash would spank me wider awake,
And made me think I'd slept through those four years
Back home in Indiana. There, landlocked, I'd breathed in,
Each day, dust from dry fields as I drove
Back roads to and from the capitol, my lungs
Nearly full, two vacuum bags choked with ashes.
Nothing I'd promised had come to pass; no one
Took a chance. I never did what I had to do.
Last year, I turned seventy-two, then pushed off

From a rickety dock moored to African earth
In a thirty-foot craft. I was the last man in waters wide
As Mars. At dusk, the sun went down, a fireball
Burning the line that stitched the sky
To sea like lit gasoline. It would glow
Above the horizon's rim long after moonlight
Fell, glimmering amid whitecaps and western waves.

344

When the sails drooped and the moon anchored
Overhead, I'd nap on my back, waiting
For wind and rain to crack the night. Once,
I woke to a vortex of white and black swirling
Round the boat, sucking it
Inward while waterfalls belted mast, tackle, and flapping
Canvas; I hugged the jib and held my breath, bricks
Of saltwater tumbling all over. Somehow,
I survived the weather's wish to turn me into
Jetsam. Dawn came, and once again flying fish
Gave signs of life and I was on the move
Cooking oatmeal and coffee, trimming
Sails, mopping deck, fidgeting with depth charts
Or sextants–always moving, always looking for wind
To shift, for sharks to surge, for land to meet
My blue unblinking eyes.

                    So now, back home
Again, I'm bored; things seem the same as ever.
And yet at night, if deep sleep comes, I dream
Lucid dreams, about sleek fish surfing
Through keyholes of reef, water currents streaming
Down their gills like air lifting the light wings
Of a Cessna whose pilot guides it beyond the clouds.

SEEING IN THE DARK   345

Below my father's house lies a river valley
where the Mississippi rolls, lifting mist
in the morning till sunlight consumes it,
slowly, the way dogs dally round dishes
when watched. At night, barge-warnings
echo up the bluff and die on our doorstep.
Sometimes, if the moon strikes you right,
and the cold air smells clean, the night pulls
you inward before you can stop
and, as you're swallowed, turns
you inside out—there

     in darkness
blindness becomes sight, and you see
how the world looks to those dying,
before first dawn light, when the moon
is glowing like a darkroom lamp
and the landscape is a negative,
undeveloped, waiting for
immersion.

PROHIBITION

In Ben Shahn's Depression mural, Feds force
foaming beer from sixteen-gallon kegs down
an open drain. It flushes through the city's sewers
and mixes with rainwatered muck that runs
into the river, whose black, viscous surface
suds at night like mugs of Guinness stout.

Ben Shahn leaves the rest untold: the Feds
lowering their fedoras' brims and sidling
from afternoon light into the dark booths
of some back-alley joint, its windows boarded,
its door unmarked like bottles they pass back
and forth. At home, my grandmother–divorced
and poor but lifelong loyalist of Hoover's ilk–
sips her last glass of bathtub gin, then makes

her first and final radical move: she'll throw
her vote to Roosevelt, and vows never again
to swill near-beer at Bevo Mill–but never
forgot those nights when, under stars, she danced
away her sober youth in the arms of men
with chests like beer barrels, empty and dark.

SHIFTWORK, IN FEBRUARY, AT TERRE HAUTE COKE AND CARBON

In winter, the cranes start eating
the mounds of black coke while it's still
dark out. On morning so cold their numb tires
turn like blocks of ice, the smokestacks,
cough up inky columns of snot and spit,
and the train tracks that vein the grounds
throb already under gauze strips of frost.
Even coal cars, empty at midnight, squat
hunchbacked with half-loads by the open docks.

Meanwhile, across the road, a small graveyard
glows in the refrigerated air; tombstones
shine like typewriter keys used to punch out
the morning obits. But now, they're as white
with untouched snow as blank newsprint waiting
for someone to make a lasting impression.

348   PREHEATING

Midsummer, heat lingers like flannel in the dusk,
beading Martini glasses with sweat. We touch
our drinks together, lightly, so they clink
like strangers at an airport grazing suitcases.

We forget the gas grill preheating on the porch,
new potatoes and green beans on the stove;
all we know is desire, all we feel is the warmth
waiting in the other's grasp. There is no tomorrow,

just now. Upstairs, like passengers, we don't look
down on what we left below, coals glowing within the dark
like distant cities; nor to what awaits us—missed
connections, ruined dinners. No, instead we fly

into a banquet of flesh, blackening our bodies
on the grills of each other's bones, like Cajun fillets
cooked fast on high heat, but eaten slow.

THE THREE-BAGGER

Like clockwork, when the crickets began to chitter
And winds vacuumed the malt of humidity from the air,
My grandfather'd cart a stool from the kitchen
To the dark corner where the radio still squats.
He'd crouch low, cupping his deaf ear as if it hurt,
And would strain, in a trance, to hear
The perpendicular thwack
Of swung wood and rawhide connecting…

Just once, on a sandlot, before his twelfth birthday,
He cracked a corkball with a broom handle so far
He forgot to run at first, it felt so good,
And still made a three-bagger, standing up.
The oldest of eight, he was drafted to fix
Sockets and lights before he saw his first curve
And so could only listen while his brothers
Broke in with clubs in the 3-I League,
And one of them, one summer, made it with Cleveland.

I imagine him still listening, even now,
Crouched upstairs above the vent in the wall:
On the mound in the basement with the count
Full, I lob the dog's ball, underhand,
To "Willie McGee," my four-year-old-boy:
He becomes a transparent eyeball blending
His swing with the pitch—and as long
As the sound lasts—connecting us all.

Mark Maire '78

A native of Oskaloosa, Iowa, Mark Maire came to
Grinnell College from the Minneapolis suburbs. Twice
he won first prize in the Selden Whitcomb competi-
tion, Grinnell's annual award for the best student
poetry. An M.A. in library science from the University
of Iowa launched Mark's career as a reference librarian.
For the past 16 years he has lived in Duluth, in the
proximity of Lake Superior and in close touch with the
drastically changing seasons in northern Minnesota.

Mark Maire's poetry has appeared in *Descant*,
Farmer's Market, *The Wolf Head Quarterly*, *Birmingham
Poetry Review*, and *The Arizona Quarterly*. His work is
full of starkly expressive, sometimes disquieting images
with abundant metaphoric resonance. A phrase from
one of his poems here–"clarity's dark, turbulent
power"–fairly describes a quality that distinguishes the
poems themselves.

HAWKS' WINGS

The sudden flash and turn
Of the speckled wings of hawks
As they dive through night air
Across roads of bleached white rock
Into roadside ditches,
Their eyes a topaz gleam,
Reminds me of those private acts
Performed inside the mind,
Those sudden turns of the will–
Momentous, but never seen–
And how the unimaginable
Is understood in an instant
Like some beautiful creature
Set immediately before us;
Or some resplendent lake
Set cold and high in the pines,
Its fathomless blue depth
A quarry already mined,
The elaborate pattern
Of our lives a tale
Already told.

352

MARCH

Straight and spare as the letter of the law,
The furrows lie fallow, making ready
For the earliest fruits, their greenest hour.
This is the month of all expectation,
The day of the hidden truths which bear fruit,
The month of immaculate conception.
The midnight sky carries within itself
An inner fire of concentration–
Promise of a great, continual flowering.
I long for the reddest rose of summer
Whose strict beauty utters all my pain,
Its blossoming the measure of all things.

HAUNTED

Here even now where these two roads converge
In a winter wood, I still think of you—
At midnight, the coldest night of the year.

In winter the memory runs deepest,
Bringing to bear the long-forgotten things:
You, the troubling cloud that has never left.

The pines by day leave long shadows on snow,
But now in the dark all colors have merged…
I think I see your face between each tree.

Overhead there is only this black sky:
Strong, immaculate, fit to be worshipped.
On the farthest star I would forget you.

354

FIRST APARTMENT: DUBUQUE, IOWA

for Dennis

In an immense Victorian window,
I placed a box fan to draw in cool air
From the river bluffs behind the building,
The coolness pent up, as if in a cave.
Yellow walls foretold a sunny future.

Evenings, at first, I walked the streets alone
Or went to an old downtown theater
Where burgundy velvet first hid the screen.
Down the block, I would reach for a locked door:
Inside, music played; people laughed and talked.

Later, we would climb spiral staircases
That hugged the bluffs, planning our bright futures,
Making a pact of undying friendship.
Reflections of Catholic steeples glimmered
On the surface of the river below.

Midnights, we entered a secret enclave
Through an alley door, made toasts, clinked glasses.
It was a private place just for our kind,
A basement underworld unknown to most,
A clandestine realm charged with potential.

In the river flats, a complex network
Of railroad tracks went in all directions,
Offering so many places to go.
In the slaughterhouse, pigs squealed and squirmed.
With a turn of the deadbolt, I was home.

Upland, rich green fields, criss-crossed everywhere
By ribbons of gravel, beckoned to us.
A poison that would not leave you alone
Soon coursed through your veins. In a slaughterhouse
Of a different kind, your mind and body
Were pummeled and ground to fine bone meal.

355

SOLSTICE

Darkness comes as early as 4:00
and, like a poison, fills the bloodstream.
I reach into my grab bag of passions,
but they're squelched, severed, ready for hanging:
a shriveled festoon on the basement line.
Neighbors on walks have gone under the hood,
shrouded like nuns or executioners,
muffled hellos mingling with falling snow.
Cars on the street are dark barges with lights
on a slow river of gunmetal gray.

In dreams, plaintive voices are barely heard
as snow fills to the brim our narrow beds.
On the rare clear night, a hint of daybreak
is the slit of light at the horizon
where, by day, grain elevators rise up
from the bay, their sleek, crystalline spires
illuminati explaining the text,
telling us what it means. Gulls pick at things,
disturbing the shore, diffusing borders,
aware by noon of the coming dark.

CLEARING AND COLDER

Moored in banks of clouds, the endless week passed,
And in drab kitchens, grievances were aired
In muffled monotone, all heard before.
Every emotion passed through a sieve,
Ending up in jars of murky water.
Country radio sang of faithless love
In lamentation straight from the Bible,
But the voice sounded tinny and enclosed.
The air smelled of wet wool, bit at our eyes.
We tumbled on mats, yet still somehow bruised.

Though some reviled him out of disdain
Or even love, to bring down the tyrant
Ruling the skies we needed evidence,
But the truth would not come out; all reports
Were vague whitewash and hagiography.
Even if we toppled him and woke up
To the startling light of a clear morning,
How would we manage the fear of blue skies,
The shock of fair weather? How would we cope
With clarity's dark, turbulent power?

358   *Stephen Kern '82*

Born on a U.S. military base in Japan, Stephen Kern had the pillar-to-post upbringing typical of an "Air Force brat": Italy, Guam, and all around the United States. When he landed in Grinnell, Kern majored in English and philosophy, graduated Phi Beta Kappa, and made no bones about wanting a career as a school teacher. After an M.A. at the University of Chicago he was immediately hired to teach English at New Trier Township High School in Winnetka, Ill. He is presently chair of the English department at William J. Palmer High School in Colorado Springs, where he teaches creative writing, the Bible as literature, and world literature in the International Baccalaureate program, an opportunity for highly motivated students. He also serves as an examiner, curriculum developer, and a teacher trainer. Married and a father of two children, Steve finds time to play piano and compose/arrange for a jazz quintet called JetStream.

Though it has won him first prize in the 1992 "Poetry West" poetry contest, Kern is modest about his poetry–which has a sneaky, sometimes playful but wry surrealistic quality. He regards himself unapologetically as first and foremost a teacher, a line of work about which he finds it hard "not to get a bit grandiloquent." "Though, hey," he thinks to add, "I can do the tired voice of realism and despair, too, when absolutely necessary."

IOWA LURKING

I almost swim
over the cooling street.
The dew teases my feet
into action.
The moon is high and bright so
I keep to the peeling
walls, under the eaves.
Across the grass
in the garden
the watermelon
is alive
in my hands before
I snap its thick vine.

A switch clicks, a light spills
over the backyard.
I am cautious but
my elbows itch in the dirt.
I try to measure
the rhythm of heat lightning so
I can make my getaway.

The backdoor leans a thin scream
into the night. If I
look up,
I will be frozen. The silence
of crickets batters the back yard. The watermelon
is dying in my hands. Elms
root against me,
I am doomed.

360
Even though this town has no dogs,
two of them bay in the distance:
we know you
we know who you are

If I remain calm perhaps the soft ground
will take me in but
I cannot be sure and cannot
leave the watermelon
behind. I test
the wind moving fitfully
east. White
flashlight washes the garden,

touches my hand. To run
and fall means brief shame
in a small town.
To give up
would be worse. I imagine

a ditchful of cattails and luck.

DREAMS FROM THE HALLWAY   **361**

I
A young boy's voice on the telephone.
Good news.
Seventeen patients here are getting better.

Technicians pass among the wheelchairs like waiters.
The doctors are being paid at last.

We await the arrival of nurses
with their long, soft hands that touch us,
bathe us, remind us of genetic successes.

II
She remembers watching an old woman–*there but
for the grace of God*–in the supermarket,

carefully opening a dark blue handbag,
extracting a Big Ben alarm clock,

speaking gently into its hands,
Come pick me up, I am alone.

If there is no answer,
she will have to pay like everyone else.

III
The temperature settles for no records today.
The gray slop in the street cakes headlights
and windshields with month old black snow water.

362

The drivers cannot see her,
cannot see the road in front of them,
and a hundred pedestrians are slaughtered.

She rests among the mangled corpses,
drawing pictures in the dark snow
so the police will know what has happened.

IV
She is most alive when traveling among the islands,
but this is not the proper season. She remembers from school:

all novels begin and end telling the whole story,
mending their brittle bones between white pages,

held together by a spine of
the latest manufacture. She finds time

to read of the South Pacific, a young boy
growing whiskerless among poinciana and breadfruit.

But she always awakens in the same hallway, living
on the same linoleum surfaces, longing
for the stiff sheets to change to white sand,

for the surgeons to leap like Polynesians
under a perpetual noon of tropical clouds.

THIS HAS NO NAME

There are poems of uncertain origin:
they might live in tight
corners and come if you call
them nasty names. You can

write them if the moon is heavy
and low to the ground.
Shove them under the bed:
they grow dark and fat

feeding on the dustballs.
Sometimes you'll wish
you had a stronger leash. Or
maybe even a whip and a chair.

And sometimes, when your mother
comes to tuck you in,
there's no way to make them
be quiet.

You just pray that the crickets outside are louder.

DIVIDE
for Joe, whatever he's up to

Watch how you remember this:

This high up, the air spreads out,
molecules seeking elbow room.
We're on our way to places we don't belong,
alien worlds, rocks old as the moon,
the light touching our skin
deadly as the rays in prehistory
before atmosphere had gathered itself together.

To disappear in a landscape like this
is a confirmation of nothing
we can find in language.
This culture of contour and ridge,
shadow and scree, refuses words
for their lack of shape,
their shallow tenuousness.

In the end, all they can do is echo.

The ice chunk from Bear Lake you grip
so I can snap its picture, clearer than air,
an invisible diamond fist numbing your hand,
refracts the stupid gaze of our questions into guesses.
This high up, two thousand feet above us still to go,
color is more geometry than physics,
more plane than particle, and nothing so gentle as wave.
Fields of snow-ice, rock-shard, sky-cloud

empty the trail into voiceless altitude.

If you can teach the lenses of your eyes
a language that knows only verbs, if you can
catalyze memory's chemicals just right,
the way back here will find you–
not the other way round:

Years later, at your desk, surrounded
by neat stacks of bills and domestic architecture,
crafting the perfectly worded memo,
you'll look up, middle-aged at last,
blurred by mid-western humidity
and the trembling nightwash of crickets,

and there, suddenly, yawns the mid-air chasm,
the eye's flight across time,
switchback, talus slope, tight spill of wildflower:

paintbrush, fireweed, columbine.

LEAF LUST

Atop the right speaker–
the one that flows the flute through *Water
Music*–Charlie, creeping Charlie (*glechoma*

hederacea), struggles to get to June (*ulmus rubra*),
the elm tree outside every
west window.

Charlie is ambitious.
Beyond the measure of his clay pot,
he reaches his fuzzy new green growth toward June,

even though we turn him every few hours or so.
Charlie's a lover, believes
with every ounce

of chlorophyl that if
we just water him enough, he can
touch June's leaves and make botanical history.

The Guide to North American Plants contains no provision
for his fervently lithesome,
leafy lust.

Still, night and day, June breathes
the even breath of trees, decades-slow,
leans ample branches toward the sky, forever

playing hard to get.

"IT IS UNLAWFUL TO DUPLICATE THIS KEY"   367

it is unlawful to duplicate this key / it is unlawful to
think about duplicating this key / it is a mortal sin in
parts of the catholic heaven to duplicate this key / it is
immoral to duplicate this key / atheistic to duplicate
this key / worse than broken flowerpots and dead
geraniums to duplicate this key / it is a cruel hoax to
duplicate this key / it is more than you know to
duplicate this key / it is the goal of all things to
duplicate this key / it is better than bread to duplicate
this key / it is the feeling of shade to duplicate this key /
it is laughter in raintime to duplicate this key / it is the
space between notes in a solo by Miles to duplicate this
key / poetry before language / rhyme before sound / it
is the main idea of this poem to duplicate this key / it is
whatever it is to duplicate this key / it makes me guilty
and free to duplicate this key / it is a bullet passing near
the heart to duplicate this key / you look and suddenly
you're someone to duplicate this key

                               that would be finding out what
this key means / that would mean opening to the table
of contents and seeing nothing but white space and the
bones of a small bird / that would mean trusting your
cat with the bones of a small bird to find out what this
key means / that would mean holding the bones up to
the light and seeing everyone's secret / that would mean
rifling the closet for a pair of clear answers / that would
mean kicking the leaves before they have fallen / or
fitting your fist in a jar of cool eels / praying for
canyons of touch / a fool's rush of trigger fish / the

368

color of coral in dreams / the lives of black holes / the
guess of this poem / the grammar of song / so /
duplicate this key / you know it exists / bet money and
trinkets / bet the moon and the stars / the orbit of love
/ the tides of abstraction / the physics of why

Martha Silano '83   369

What the Truth Tastes Like (Nightshade Press), Martha
Silano's first book of poems, won the William &
Kingman Page Poetry Book Award for 1998. She
received her M.F.A. degree from the University of
Washington and currently teaches English at Edmonds
Community College in Lynnwood, Wash. As one
might gather from her poetry, Martha's experiences and
enthusiasms are wide-ranging; she lists her previous
occupations as "hay-baler, artist's model, fruit picker,
proofreader, CPS caseworker, legal assistant, and book
reviewer."

Martha Silano has been a fellow at the Millay
Colony for the Arts, Dorland Mountain Arts Colony,
the Virginia Center for the Creative Arts, and the
University of Arizona Poetry Center. She is represented
by several poems included in an anthology titled
American Poetry: the Next Generation scheduled for
publication in the spring of 2000 by Carnegie Mellon
University Press. Her work has appeared in *Artful
Dodge*, *Crab Creek Review*, *The Florida Review*, *Hanging
Loose*, *The Paris Review*, *Poetry Northwest*, *Verse*, and on
the Seattle Metro bus line. To pick up on that vehicular
reference, reading Martha's poems can be a bit like a
ride on a carnival tilt-a-whirl. Except that–if you
manage to hang on while the language and allusions
take you through some wild and willful crack-the-
whip–one of the rewards in addition to the exhilarating
trip itself is a sense of arrival.

370   A TRIP THROUGH THE YELLOW PAGES:
BA, BE, AND SO FORTH

We begin with Babbitting, Beckwith & Kuffel, then quickly
move on to Babies: Tot Stoppers, breast pumps, Lifetime

Furniture. There's Stork Express, Go to Your Room,
merry-go-rounds and Pre-Learning Inc.,

but before we get the scoop on in-the-womb
teaching, we're on to backflow, Badge Express,

Button King. What next? Burlap.
Who are we calling? Lacey O'Malley, Bail Bondsman.

Where to? Both Ways Catering. "Everything She Touches
Tastes Terrific," the ad for LUV-N-OVN says, "Just Dial EAT-

CAKE," and we will, but we must move on to Balemaster, True
    Wheel,
Large Capacity Portable Stands, we must pick a barrel to hold

our waste, choose from the largest selection of towel bars
in the West. Then on to Aurora for retail, wholesale, Life

Plus, then smack in the middle of bushings, bearings,
cowplugs–which brings us to Beauty (sheaves

to shears)–Adam & Eve, A Cut Above, Connie
and her Class Act. Now that we're weaved and braided,

coiffed and permed, trimmed and waxed, now that acrylic
adorns our nails (two weeks guaranteed), we find ourselves

in Adjustable Beds, Quality Down for 50 Years, Comforter
Kits. Let us Sit-N-Sleep, then let us be lifted

from our remote control rest (factory direct),
past idlers, pulleys and PVC to the heaven

of Prompt Response and champagne fountains.

372   FOR A FRIEND WHO SENDS ME
          A FLYER ON THE ART OF EAR CANDLING
          AND NEWS HER BOOK HAS ARRIVED

Could it be true? That a hollow taper,
poised at the edge of an ear, ignited,
sucks out years of "interesting contents"?
Drawn by a narcissistic longing to see
your own wax, would you risk a loss of hearing?
Swabs, it says, are detrimental, cannot reach
the depths. "Upon inspection," would the flame extrude,

in the form of mites, your mother the harbinger's *honey,*
the belt goes around your waist...blue side down;
does your father's *yastupiddummydon'tgivemeanyofyourguff*
swell like fungus the size of a brain coral? What about his
don't be talkin, which lodged itself in a clump so thick
(in the oval window? in the bony labyrinth?) it echoes
your every word? What if it *did* loosen (gently,

with crackling, with hissing) every fluid movement,
every cumulonimbus-shaped incus vibration,
every ounce of sound within thirty-three years
of earshot? Could you have it pick and choose?
Could you rig it, for instance, so it only softens
the good stuff, the *You, Yes YOUs!*? Could you have it
skip the refusals, *the let's just be friends,*
Mr. Hoppel's lawnmower drowning out the robins
at dusk, Bobby Whitman's Chevy the 99 times before
it turned over? What is wax but food for flame?

And you're waxing, Debi. This is the time
to pick corn, Whitman's "full-noon trill,"
the time to let loosen amber kernels
of grief, your time to shine.
Rolled in your ears the ancient waxing–
Goddess Diana–rolled in your ears
what's kept our friendship incandescent
(two cradled receivers, two lobed doubloons).

But "Oy!!!!!!!" your letter cries
(every bird that sang singing again).
You heard stomping, a loud knock,
then leapt for the door; your voice gleamed
over seven machines before it hit you: *this is mine,*
this my own. Book you know like the lines ringing
your mouth, lines of sound, vibrating bone. How small
the part we see (squiggles and curlicues sway
where a Q-tip never dreamed). One tube's named
for Bartolommeo Eustachio; there's a vestibule,
a stirrup, a drum (the mind flickers with all
it cannot know); the tragus barely tells
the prologue...

I'm tempted, Debi–tempted to "feel a lightness
in the head," to use it as an ancient stenographer:
"to write upon wax laid on boxwood, to form,
with an iron stylus":

374   OF COURSE YOUR EARS ARE BURNING!

But what if this candling did do damage?
Turned *rapport* to *purulence*?
Made what we've pigeon-holed disappear,
left us with only the *hroo-hroo* of doves?

Notice how this Chris Coppens Coons, Certified
Candler, makes no reference to sticking or spearing,
to lancing or drilling, to dirking, plunging, forcing
or spiking, but mentions only "receiving" massage,
"involving" the use of a candle...

Nope. We can't risk it. Can't give up
how we hear a song first (mother, father,
yellow-rumped warbler...), then rout out
the body. Nor the chance to strain our ears
for the heart of a baby long before he swims
the canal. Can't risk losing the riff and jam
of our whole-balla-wax, can't-hold-a-candle-to
jags. Like two Black Turbans we cling
to what's shaped us—held by the roar of the sea.

WHAT I MEANT TO SAY
BEFORE I SAID "SO LONG"
for Dante Alfredo Silano

There will be spiders the size of your ears, drinks
that will make you stupid, matches you'll long
to strike; there will be mop-ups the size of Rhode Island.

Or you'll be driving at night beneath the cloud-hidden Perseids
but the car in front will lose a wheel, spray a million sparks.
The spider won't drop its strand above your bed,

but choose a far corner. Don't kill it.
What it spins will rival what (dewfully, sparklingly) hangs
from your neighbor's hedge. Your father loves

what shines—the flash in the pan, two-penny nugget
glint, what might lead him from buckets, latex, brush's
swish, loves the gleam that was you

in his eye. As a child he built fires beneath a rising
Dog Star, ignored the heat, his mother's no's,
heard only "go ahead, Matty-boy, my Tee-too, my Shaver, build

whatever you like." Loved what was left
when the brightness died, to fish the yard
for the stubs of rockets. What he kindled in Ash Flat—

eight miles from Evening Shade, the lift of earth
that is Ozarks—he feeds logs to now (last stop
before the flashing CHAINS REQUIRED), where the spark

376   between him and your mother...where you were born.
       Ashland. Which must be why they named you
       Dante, an unlit match held close

       to a blaze, what it means to burn like hope.
       He pans for gold, tells us by the crow's fly (by the eagle,
       by the osprey), we're close to a mine, scars

       in the side of a hill, close to where the flood of '64
       tore the earth, unearthed the glimmers he dreams of.
       He's got scars on his back and stretches of road

       he can't recall, but don't be scared: all that firewater's
       behind him, the bottomless tap, beer after golden beer....
       His love for explosives cost him all the gold

       in the Applegate Valley, "Possession of a Firearm" emblazoned
       on screens from Metuchen to Tucson–"a pellet gun; I shot
       at the sky..." (not that we're here

       forever, not that we don't live
       in the shadow of live volcanoes, the chance
       we'll wake to at least a dusting

       of ash). "So long, trooper,"
       I managed to say, your father asking
       for Roman Candles, Dancing Bees, Flower Clusters,

       "stuff that shoots out sparks." South of Eugene,
       two hundred miles from your eager hands,
       the sun through clouds a million motionless searchlights,

I began to fall in a trap. *Don't let boredom grip you*   377
the way you gripped my finger. Let even the seemingly
starkest places yield you black-eyed susans. Learn

from the woman who with her entire body tells you,
"I've done all this." Since each of us will soon
be part of the meal, since we're more like tents

than mountains, and mountains disappear...
(spinning...sinking...fuel light
an ember...finally sputtering out).

378

TOO SMALL FOR INTELLECT,
BIG ENOUGH FOR LOVE
*—early 20th century obstetrics text
describing a woman's brain*

My grandmother wasn't a chemist, but in her kitchen I learned
precision, science of dollop, pinch. She didn't own

a thermometer, measured heat with a dab to her wrist.
Yeast foamed like the incoming tide at Love Ladies beach,

like drops of HCl on a test tube filled with zinc. Kneaded not
by machine so that now I can't enter my kitchen, touch

bowl, sugar, flour, wooden spoon without her long-earned
confidence dissolving the shame of a hundred chem lab flops—

scales so sure weight changed with a breeze, easily broken pipets,
terror of Bunsen burner, meniscus more a reason

to pause (that water could smile like that!). Without her hands
on mine *feel how that feels? Now you're ready for rising…*

TOWARD AN UNDERSTANDING
OF MY SO-CALLED CALLING

It's my mother's fault.
When I squirmed in church,
craned to count, on the bridges

of stern parishioners, horn-rims
and cat eyes; when I looked up,
not in search of light or truth,

but to fill the wooden beams
with loopy, imagined script;
when her glance, which I'm sure

could stop them now, failed to stop
my swinging legs, she'd grab her purse
(an eye on me, an eye on the priest),

dig past needles, rows of knit and purl,
lipstick bright as flamingos, ubiquitous
tissues, the silvery rain hat

folded down and down
to one thick, snapped down strip,
hand me paper and pen.

Blame my father, post-cookout
star-gazer, astronomically
enthusiastic ("lots of kids

380

have burgers; how many Seven Sisters?"),
who taught the comfort of wandering Cassiopeia.
The ones that moved, he said, were ours.

Blame them both, their painstaking passions—
infinitesimal, all-consuming, pointless
as too-far-off-to-warm-us stars,

as a great, great, grandmother's tightly woven
bun, which though I never saw it,
was rumored to fall to her knees.

SPELLCHECK CHANGES *SILANO* TO *SALINE*

but I don't mind—ever-
tearful, ever-nicknamed
Pickles Queen. Lover
of brine—splash zone,
pelagic, sublittoral. Home
where the ocean's near.
Ever drawn to the true point
of beginning—horseshoe crabs
on a Wildwood beach,
crinoid lilies swaying shallowly.
What, after all, is *Silano*?
Father's father's father's…
18 *greats* to Senator Eppio,
richest of Roman blood,
but just one quarter,
while under a tugging sea—
Katrosh, Bullock, Pickarski…
Mother's maiden name, please (underside
of who we are, shadow self,
whispering). With a name like Saline
maybe I'd befriend the crepuscular
thick knees, glimpse magellanic plover's
bright Chilean feet. Rise each dawn
to the probing marks of sanderlings
while floating up from the surf the almost-
audible tunes of murmuring sirens—
bulka, kapusta, shushpie. Might ease the final trip
to Graveyard Spit ashes scattered
near sticky daisy, sand verbena, rocket pea,
bill of the ever-pirouetting phalarope…

Anne Vilen '83

After college, where she majored in English and philosophy, Anne Vilen spent several years doing editorial work for *Partisan Review* in Boston, for *Signs: Journal of Women in Culture and Society* in Durham, and for The University of North Carolina Press at Chapel Hill (where she earned a master of arts in teaching degree). Moving to Denver, Anne taught English composition and creative writing in a number of academic posts and, she says, "began to really explore and nurture my own creative process." Back again in North Carolina, Anne has well and truly gone into business for herself as a writer and teacher of writing. Self-employed as "The Write Woman," she performs stories and teaches creativity and writing workshops for arts councils, public schools, elderhostels, women's centers, retreats, and hospitals across the country. Inspired by those whom she inspires, Anne Vilen has published poems and essays in journals and magazines including *High Plains Literary Review*, *Women's Studies Quarterly*, *Common Boundary*, *Poets and Writers Magazine*, and the *Washington Post Sunday Magazine*. She is co-editor of *Sisters and Workers in the Middle Ages* (University of Chicago Press, 1989). She lives now in Cullowee, N.C., with her husband Bill Kwochka '83, who teaches chemistry at Western Carolina University, and their two children.

Contemporary women writers, especially those who both write poems and raise children, have been a

sustaining influence (Anne mentions Lucille Clifton,
Naomi Shihab Nye, Linda Hogan, and Sharon Olds).
"These poets help me to figure out how catching
fireflies with my children, listening to a cancer survivor
tell her story, and writing poems in a small Appalachian
town can all be the same meaningful work." That work
and also Anne's strong evocative powers and a born
storyteller's sense of pace and timing are evident in her
poems.

384   THE BATH

When I was twelve
and just coming into my own sex,
I shared a pink bathroom
with four older sisters.

Behind the locked door,
I peered through the second-story window
to watch the neighbor kids
kick-the-can into evening without me.
I didn't mind.

Inside
on the toilet lid, Gwen's eyelash curler,
an open box of tampons,
cotton smeared with black mascara,
a rosy compact blushing against white porcelain
marked the territory with a scent no girl could mistake.

Water rising in the claw-footed tub,
I let myself sink down and drown,
holding my breath under the water
til I could feel my long hair feign
the feathered tresses of a lion's mane.
And other hairs, new tufts,
where I was just beginning to feel the roar.

Gail had taught me the alchemy of shine.
I swirled the pearl cream rinse
with water in a red plastic tumbler,

conjuring the blonde Breck girl on the dream screen,
letting her fingers stream over my brow,
my neck, smacking my lips with the cool of it.

The water draped me smooth as pale silk
a white skin of silk over a ripple of ribs
and the soft-spoken tumescence of new breasts
shivering like acacia leaves in the hot air.

I pulled the plug and let the water run between my legs,
watching the dusky suds subside and the fur rise.
There on the steaming plain of the bath I found
my self, new as morning on the savanna.
Lithe, limber, wild.

AFTER MOTHER DIED

When I was twelve
a boy across the county
fell through the February ice
and lived under the water
for more than twenty minutes.
They pulled him out, alive, but
blue as a frozen trout with his hands open
and fingers extended like fragile fins.

For months after that
I imagined how he must have
pulled himself deeper and deeper
into the winter light
into the cold comfort of the lake's womb
into the dream where webbed hands weave ribbons of water.

And I pretended to be that boy
trekking alone each evening
through the slush and snow
to find myself at the local recreation center
with its Olympic-sized pool anchored in the basement.

Graceful as a sea turtle
my long braids streaming like seaweed
I dove beneath the lane lines
and pulled my hands
webbed like his, pink as pearls
through the watery world.
Lifting and rolling

curving and sculling   **387**
I conjured myself the flukes of a fragile
sea creature and felt my way back in time
marked only by the motion
of fingers feathered with delicate, glistening bubbles.

Caught in the hush
of the pool's drowned floodlights
my shadow angled deeper
into the blue bottomless dome
into the drumming desire of my nascent life
into the wet-warm wash of my mother's womb
restful, rolling, and round
sensual, soulful, and sound.

Down there
breathing under the water
I felt my life return to me.

MOTHER CROW

I
Yesterday
an explosion of crows met us at the alley gate,
hurling threats and warnings like beaked bullets
from the phone wire, garage eaves, the lowest branch of
    the linden.
Wanting desperately to shut them out–
the noise, the heat, the frightening shadows lurking
    overhead–
I cowered.
But not my newborn daughter.
Condensing her eight pounds into a mask of sound
menacing and sharp as a cleaver,
she screamed back,
scattering those crows like scraps of ash.

II
Today
the crows still hunch on the wire,
three of them with steady eyes stuffed into slick black
    dusters.
But I see, suddenly, that this is a vigil of protection, not
    menace.
Their ruffled fledgling–a fuzzy, awkward echo of its
    parents–
blunders over a drain pipe and stubs its nose on the
    garden wall.
With criminal patience, two cats wait under the picnic
    table, tails flicking.

Stretching his striped claws forward, orange cat is **389**
a burglar, belly down, muscles tensed, eyes on his prize.
Dispassionate as any neighbor
I watch this beastly drama unfold.
Mother Crow's brash voice shatters the air, and
shielding the fragile architecture of her wings
with talons and beak like bayonets,
she strafes the wary cat.
The cat retreats and waits, eyes dangerous as blades.
And the crows reconvene their watch, mindful
of the power pounding beneath wings.
Meanwhile, the frightened fledgling closes its eyes,
dreaming of air and green branches
and the deadly threat of cats miniaturized by flight.

III
Now, sitting at my breakfast table,
newsprint flaps from the bright page into my brain:
"On Friday morning a 23-year-old woman was forced
        at gunpoint...
at 10:35 a.m. and ordered into an alley. While aiming a
        gun at the
woman's head, the attacker forced her to pull down her
        pants and
lay on the ground. The man then inserted a knife in the
        woman's
vagina, telling her, 'Make a sound and you die.' The
        attacker fled by
running north in the alley."

390

IV

Always
I imagine it happening to her,
happening to me,
happening to my daughter,
happening to every woman.
Nearby
a shadow slides out from behind a dumpster
clutches her arm with dirty claws,
drags her toward the alley, fighting.
Gun barrel bores the crime into her skull.
He pushes her against the hot asphalt,
sucking the air from her chest.
Her body collapses—
hissed into silence,
a gutted fish on the griddle.
The sharp edges of gravel carve his intentions into her
        spine.
A knife gleams in the sun like silver in the palm of a
        thief.
The blade creases her thighs
and she plummets deep into a sudden black erasure.
Closing her eyes against the hulking weight of
what is happening to her
she floats skyward into a dream of air and green
        branches.
She is flying.
Sunlight.
The weight gone now,
and footsteps running to the beat of the blood pound-
        ing in her temple.

V

When the newsprint gathers once again into the shape
    of letters,
my chest is heaving.
Natal power and mother madness drum in my veins.
The bones of my ankles split and lengthen into talons.
My elbows web out and up into sinewed wings.
My skin sprouts a dark, oiled plumage.
My face narrows and sharpens.
My chin and nose fuse into a razor-like barb.

Furious and ferocious, I fly from this cage
finding at last the strength to crash down and peck out
    eyes
the vision to see I am much more than my size
the desire to take all women under my wing
the courage to join my daughter, my sisters
and the dangerous, defiant Mother Crow
SCREAMING
IN THE RIGHTEOUS, ANGRY AIR

392   TAKING THE CURE IN RESERVE, MONTANA

This place welcomes me like the reaching arms
of a plains woman too long without a knock on her door.

Fewer than a dozen houses,
skitter in the hot wind--
beetles overturned in the long grass,
chimneys wriggling.

Across the tracks a yellowed hound
chases my tires. The same one nipped my heels,
raised above the fenders of a Schwinn,
twenty years, twenty lifetimes ago.

I park on the old foundation
beside her house where
someone has planted a basketball hoop on a pole.
It prays like a mantis over the cracked cement.

In the neighbor's yard, cotton sheets crack and ricochet
against the clothesline like corn popping.
The neighbor waves from behind her laundry
as if she knows me, as if she wants to.

My grandmother's yard is overgrown with prairie vetch
and buffalo grass. Cactus crabs have crawled
down from the hills and rooted their claws
in the driveway. Against the neighbor's neat coiffure
this yard is punk-green dreadlocks.

Mounting the porch step, I kick up a railroad spike
that pings with exactly the sound of the tin ladle
rattling against the side of her porcelain drinking basin.
Once I was sure the ladle's song and the water,
mineral rich and hauled from Medicine Lake,
would cure all aches.

The house is empty four years now,
doors locked tight, windows bolted against indifferent
Canadian gales, plains dust that scours the paint.
Only the wind touches this place anymore.

And yet, pressing my face against the pane
I am sure I see a curtain flutter,
feel the breeze lift a newly crocheted doily
from the back of a kitchen chair.
I am sure I hear a Swedish creak from the pantry
"Is dat you Bett?"
smell the buttery cinnamon of fresh rolls licking my nose.
I am sure I taste the water—restorative, pure.

I swallow as deeply as an open window
and lean toward waiting arms.

Susan Sink '86

During her senior year in college Susan Sink met the
poet Edward Hirsch '72, see pp. 259–271, who was
visiting his alma mater as one of the distinguished guests
of that year's Writers' Conference. Susan refers to Hirsch's
poetry and his encouragement of her own work as "a
turning point for me." After Grinnell, while she was
earning her master of fine arts degree at Sarah Lawrence
College, Susan continued to correspond with Ed Hirsch
and to profit from his long-distance mentoring. She
attended Stanford University as a Wallace Stegner Fellow
in poetry and has been awarded residences at Yaddo and
The McDowell Colony. At present she teaches composi-
tion, world literature, and creative writing at Joliet Junior
College in Illinois. Currently seeking publication of a
collection of her poems titled *The Way of All the Earth*,
she has also turned to fiction writing and has recently
completed a novel.

Susan Sink's distinctive, memorably unsettling, yet
confident and confiding voice seems well suited both to
edge familiar subjects (new love, family relations)
toward the unexpected and to startle an interest in
unlikely ones (catching and eating frogs, the consuming
world of fundamentalist Christianity). Her work has
appeared in *Poetry*, *Chicago Review*, *Indiana Review*, and
The Journal (Ohio State University). Her poem, "The
Catch," was a prizewinner in *Salt Hill Journal*'s annual
competition.

HEALING WARTS AT CHRIST'S CHAPEL ASSEMBLY OF GOD CHURCH

The widows came on swollen legs and feet;
the pastor brought his gnarled fingers; the parents
of the lost child came with their distracted look,
the pianist with a French twist to deny the tumor.

They all came down the aisle to pray
for my teenage sister, who had warts.
They believed enough to press their hands
to hers eagerly, wanting God to knot

their joints with His strength, the sap flow
through their spotted skins on its way to heal the young.
They were filled with visions of blind eyes opened by mud
and spit and by daily t.v. miracles. They were tongued
        inarticulate with hope.

And my sister was a teenage girl who hadn't eaten
a full meal in months, or raised her hand in class,
or practiced the piano, or clapped in astonishment
or praise, or held anyone's hand, or even touched anyone.

After attempts to burn the sores away and private,
useless family prayers, we admitted our need
and called—and it was clear who answered.
I'd been afraid they would scorn the petty request,

afraid my sister would be hurt by the ordeal of this love:
stretching blemished hands to those who expected

396   miracles for their children. But it was also this simple:
their hands on her hands, their human voices.

It wasn't the healing, ever, that mattered.
It was the love, even done this poorly,
what little we could do with what the world allowed:
our battered hands and this God.

FROGLEGS

At that lake house the croaking gets in your ears
until one night you're hungry with it.

You need a snake-tongued fork, long-handled.
You need a flashlight and a canvas bag.

Your eyes adjust to the dark until you know
where to aim the light. Steady. You hear one.

Stunned, blinded, it won't move
or speak. You have that second.

Drive the fork through the center.
Don't mind if it jumps, he said,

that's reflex, not pain. He said
they're nothing but nervous system.

You know it when you strip one from fork
to bag. The way a few can jump the canvas sack

across a table. But you'll want more
than a few. The meat is meager,

the skinned creatures like giblets,
like hearts. It's only the legs you want. Remember.

The legs, too, will jump when they're severed.
But, you see, it's clear that they're dead.

398

When they're battered and fried, you almost forget
where they came from. What happened.

When you taste them they taste
like he said they would, like chicken. Better.

Their pumping bodies, the light in their eyes—
you forget. Or no, you remember, but it doesn't matter.

THE CATCH

From the sea we learned how small
    we were, but fearless, anchored
        by my grandfather, lines cast.

We could do nothing but watch
    green shadows on the choppy,
        carnivorous sea, and wait.

A baby shark was first to take my line,
    its body smooth as plastic. My grandfather
        unhooked it easily, then bent its nose

and tossed it over, where it circled
    upside down, a broken toy, its gills
        filled to drowning with unbreathable water.

Sometimes there were "garbage fish,"
    blowfish he unlocked from the hooks
        with his nine-fingered, junkman's hands.

He bounced them on the boat's bottom
    while we stood on the seats, then he flung
        the stunned scavengers back out to sea.

Flounder caught off that boat
    came so smoothly from the water,
        it was more harvest than hunt.

400   Mottled gray and flat as skipping stones,
                I imagined them skimming the sea in infinite
                        short hops, until grandfather dipped the net

          and brought them aboard. They never
                got away, so poorly adapted, both eyes
                        sunk in the same side of their heads.

          They were doubly sad, pale beggars,
                staring up at us with all they had.
                        But these were the ones we photographed,

          The helpless prizes, the meaty keepers;
                this is what we came for, the good fish,
                        lying still in the deep boxes by the seat.

TWO POEMS ABOUT
MY FATHER AND MOVIES

1

My father, at seven, realizes he can save a dime
by walking, not taking the connecting bus. He is a child,
on his way from his grandmother to mother: too far to walk.
He lifts his small suitcase and starts down the highway.
A woman offers him a ride before he tires, cries for the missed
bus, or is lost in the town that looks different on foot.
It will be this way every Saturday for years, hitching
rides to Camden with mothers nothing like his own.
On those days when he arrives to find
her not home, door locked, he has the dime,
and he and his suitcase, brown
as a man's brown hat, go to the movies.

2

My father shows such amazement when we ask
where he's going, answers "out," as though it's the first time
anyone asked him and none of his children's business.
Later I go to a movie with friends, impulsively,
one not meant for kids our age, and I pass my father
leaving the early show. It's a popular movie, but still
I'm embarrassed seeing him, being seen.
Some nights he comes home with a haircut,
a story of a softball game, or stack of library books.
But tonight we pass in the lobby like theatergoers,
and I go in and he smiles and goes out.

CODA: SUMMER ON THE DIG

At home with me, another man,
who was equally careless
with the earth, but lucky
not to chunk into anything
of value, held me as though
I could crumble beneath his touch.
All summer we worked on our courage,
driving out to the unambiguous
Indian mounds with bottles of wine,
kissing in a borrowed car on the edge
of flattened acres of yellow corn,
knowing there was much to tell,
brushing the earth gently,
trying—we were young—
to accomplish the impossible task:
to bring what is hidden to light
without disturbing it.

MERCY
Silver Lake, Michigan

It was what we'd been waiting for,
to be called from our rooms above the kitchen,
the ten Christian girls of Flora-dale Resort, called
at night from the foot of the stairs:
Trim your lamps! Come quick! It's time!

Roxanne and I had been praying for it,
a sign of the beauty we knew must be there,
just beyond our devoted efforts to find it:
the deer who appeared and disappeared
while we served breakfast to the guests,

the secret paradise too deep in the woods
to be reached on afternoon breaks,
the perfect wave breaking behind the dunes,
or the dunes themselves, shifting while we watched—
those of us worn away by that same wind:

Roxanne, who didn't tell what her father did,
what six brothers and sisters witnessed
and none stopped; Laura paling upstairs
with stacked romances, afraid to leave the room;
and me, with the small idea of my strength,

racing Roxanne to the airstrip each day for prayer.
In that swath mown clear for Ed's two-engine plane
we held hands, the same two girls we'd always been,
wanting to be good, asking to be changed.
What could we do to make this world love us?

404

What could we do to cast out our pain—
pain we'd somehow caused ourselves by accident.
Roxanne told about the fire her four-year-old self set,
that killed her three-year-old sister.
I told her what little I remembered:

my grandfather trapping me, and later
the old man who died in the restaurant,
how I went for help too late.
The truth is, as little good as God's love
seemed to be doing us, we believed in it.

We couldn't do anything right. We felt hated
and blamed by the owners of this place,
Ed and his wife Delores, who gave us a roof
and a pretty good living. I'd been praying
to learn servanthood as God meant it.

All we knew to ask for was beauty,
and we begged God at that airstrip
to reward our search—on foot, rowboat,
on the Great Lake and the small. We knew
the call was for us when it came, and ran to the beach.

I wouldn't be disappointed, even by the faint light
I wouldn't have known was aurora borealis,
the name we breathed like a kyrie eleison,
dimmer than starlight, transparent,
like the lights of a far city,

like a flotilla with its one thousand boatmen
turning flashlights to the sky. And why not that,
come silently over the water, moored behind the dunes,
come to reward our incessant hoping in the dark,
come not to bestow mercy but to ask for it.

406   *Kendra Ford '93*

For two years after graduating from Grinnell, Kendra
Ford earned her living baking bread, trained by a
"bread mystic," as she puts it, "who taught me that even
yeast has a voice in this universe." From such begin-
nings, San Francisco State University and an M.A. in
creative writing was not, perhaps, the most unlikely
next step. Since high school, however, Kendra had been
persistently drawn to a career in the ministry; accord-
ingly, she left northern California to enter the
Meadville/Lombard Universalist Unitarian Seminary,
an affiliate of the University of Chicago. Currently she
is in the final stages of her ministerial training: working
as an intern minister in Asheville, N.C.

    In addition to her master's thesis, a collection of
poems titled *A Human Temperature* (1997), Kendra's
work has appeared in several graduate program
publications and in her seminary newsletter. Does the
mingling in her poems of the stern and the wistful, the
fey and the earnest, remind anyone else of Christina
Rossetti?

LILIES

Lilies speak to no one
Roses have been bent to it
but lilies rise, thin and green,
above the daily squabblings
And when we see their open faces
turned upward
we glance up ourselves
wondering if it's light
they live on
Straining to hear how
they whisper among themselves
I have put my face to theirs
and been brushed–golden
though never spoken to.

408

WHAT DO YOU DO WHEN
YOU CAN'T STAND IT ANYMORE

I went one night, in the rain
down the rocky coast
to have my body boiled away.
Someone told me it would be purifying.
The steam and the dim lights
perched on the cliff edge.
I could smell cedar in the wind
and sulfur underneath.
The ocean air had fish-cold hands
so the hot water felt good.
I floated, a little dumpling,
it was painless
as my body began to dissipate,
salt in the soup.
I could feel my tendons
separate, begin to dissolve.
"I need to get out." I peered
into the mineral haze.
I'll tell you, by then there is nothing
you can do.
You've been released
into the dark forms of the air
and it is so painful to see the trees
longing to be out of their bark
and all the sleeping people
wanting out of their tight skins,
even the old ocean
pushing at its rocks.

NOT READY

One cloudy afternoon her heart
beat faster than she could count.
The doctor said, this happens
to hearts like hers.
Her chest ached for days, stretched.

Her cousin's baby had a heart,
not ready for this world–
it didn't beat
it opened and closed, opened and closed
opened.

She too could die of an open heart–
drown in the green of the sun soaked trees
under the swarming dark sky.
Her heart might over ripen,
a peach in the orchard,
filled, after sugar, with rain
and split its own skin.

LOSING HER BREATH

The mountains are firm under the sky
which breathes more evenly than she does.
She's still so beautiful, her hair in a knot,
her cheeks pink, her hands calm.
Lucky, he thinks, that she ever agreed.
She scrapes a breath up.
The mountains arch under their snow.
Two cups of tea and an old silver spoon
between them. He has always served.
She's begun to go away, every now and then.
He finds her absent in her apron
looking out beyond the fruit trees.

The mail comes, there's a letter.
They read it out, each of them
the words taste good.
They hold hands instead of drinking tea.
It's lonely in love.
It might be months yet, even a year
any cup could be eternity.

THIS IS HOW BREAD RISES

a cluster of grapes, a bowl of old apples
is remembered for a hundred years
a jar of this fermenting fruit is shared

turning in the mixing bowl
dough moves against the direction of the clock,
like all things which grow

the ocean, or our own blood,
nothing's right without the salt

someone remembers the dough is shining in its bowl
slowly opening spaces inside itself

as with any good dancer
you must forget who's watching
and move by feeling,
the gentle urging at your back, in your hand

hands shaping a loaf
form a wing span, thumb to thumb
so hands can learn to fly

handled and small the loaves rise again
simple things, stretching in their skins

OFFERINGS

For those who are shy but resolute, almonds and milk
and carry a smooth striped stone in your pocket.
For those who are first to speak, crisp green apples
and wear well worn hiking boots.
For those who refuse to believe, even what they see, tart
        stewed rhubarb
then greet each living thing you meet by its name.
For those whose minds will not empty, a full samovar
        of tea
while someone brushes and brushes your hair.
For those who are exhausted to emptiness, lentil soup
and watch the waves till the tide turns, then sleep.
For those who find the faces of others inscrutable, hot
        pepper jam
and sit in the front row at the movies and watch the
        audience.
For those who get lost in their own freedom, slow rising
        bread
then write on birch bark all that you believe.
For those who are surprised by their own needing, grits
        and molasses
then sit in the dim auditorium during every choir
        practice.
For those who are afraid to listen, thick simmering stew
and sit in the park until, among the bird calls, you hear
        your name.
For those who are afraid of what they must do, wild
        berry pie
and walk everywhere you go.

Poem Sources

Thanks are due to the following poets, their representatives, and publishers for permission to include certain poems in this anthology. Unless otherwise noted (or the poem is in the public domain), permission to republish came from the copyright holder.

Whicher, George Mason.

—*Lang Syne*, originally published in *The Unit* (Grinnell College).
—*To Be Forgotten*, originally published in *The Tanager* (Grinnell College), 1928.
—*I Have Forgotten Much*, originally published in *The Tanager* (Grinnell College), 1928.
—*Amity Street*, from *Amity Street and Other Light-Hearted Verse* by G. M. Whicher. The Bookmart, 1935.
—*Invitation*, from *Amity Street and Other Light-Hearted Verse* by G. M. Whicher. The Bookmart, 1935.
—*The Secret*, from *Amity Street and Other Light-Hearted Verse* by G. M. Whicher. The Bookmart, 1935.

Whitcomb, Selden L.

—*After the Theater*, originally published in *Midland Monthly*, January 1898.
—*"Questi, Che Mai Da Me Non Fia Diviso,"* originally published in *The Unit* (Grinnell College), January 1897.
—*On Wansfell Pike*, originally published in *The Unit* (Grinnell College), January 1897.
—*Rhymes of the Battlefield: Behind the Lines, The Sharp-Shooter, Spangler's Spring, Blue-Ridge, Lincoln, Peace,* originally published in *The Unit* (Grinnell College), 1897.
—*Questioning*, originally published in *The Unit* (Grinnell College), 1897.
—*The Path-Makers*, originally published in *Poetry: A Magazine of Verse*, August 1924.

Booth, Bertha May.

—*A Dream*, originally published in *The Unit* (Grinnell College), April 1897.
—*Heavenly Heights, (To Sister Mary Josephine)*, originally published in *The Unit* (Grinnell College), June 1898.
—*Opportunity*, originally published in *The Unit* (Grinnell College), December 1898.
—*Inadequacy*, originally published in *The Unit* (Grinnell College), May 1900.
—*Mountain Mist*, originally published in *The Unit* (Grinnell College), May 1900.
—*To a Water Lily*, originally published in *The Unit* (Grinnell College), 1912.

Bowen, Helen Jean.

—*Seven Sonnets*, from *Seven Sonnets* by Helen Jean Bowen, Wind-Tryst Press, Chicago, 1899.

Walleser, Joseph.

—*On Beginning Homer*, originally published in *The Unit* (Grinnell College), 1901.

—*The Eclipse*, originally published in *The Unit* (Grinnell College), June 1910.

—*To a Wren*, originally published in *The Unit* (Grinnell College), April 1912.

—*Youth, (From the French of Pascal-Bonetti)*, from *Junto* (Grinnell College), October 1924.

—*Sunset, (English version of Kroustallis's tribute to Epirus)*, originally published in *The Tanager* (Grinnell College), May 1924.

Hall, James Norman.

—*The Attack*, originally published in *The Tanager*, Vol. IV (November 1928, Grinnell College). Copyright © by James Norman Hall. Reprinted by permission of Nancy Rutgers.

—*New York, I. One Autumn Afternoon, II. From My Room in East 70th St., III. The Bread Line*, originally published in *The Tanager*, Vol. VIII (July 1932, Grinnell College). Copyright © by James Norman Hall. Reprinted by permission of Nancy Rutgers.

—*The Journey to Come*, from *O'Millersville!* published in 1941 by the Prairie Press, Muscatine, Iowa. Copyright © by James Norman Hall. Reprinted by permission of Nancy Rutgers.

—*Poetry*, from *O'Millersville!* published in 1941 by the Prairie Press, Muscatine, Iowa. Copyright © by James Norman Hall. Reprinted by permission of Nancy Rutgers.

—*The Over-Night Guests*, from *O'Millersville!* published in 1941 by the Prairie Press, Muscatine, Iowa. Copyright © by James Norman Hall. Reprinted by permission of Nancy Rutgers.

Suckow, Ruth.

—*Song in October*, originally published in *Midland*, 1918.

—*Prayer at Timber-Line*, originally published in *Poetry: A Magazine of Verse*, June 1921.

—*Beauty*, originally published in *Poetry: A Magazine of Verse*, June 1921.

—*The Odd Ones*, originally published in *Poetry: A Magazine of Verse*, June 1921.

—*Grampa Schuler*, originally published in *Poetry: A Magazine of Verse*, June 1921.

Grubbs, Verna.

—*POEMS I, Caprice, New Moon, Second Spring*, originally published in *The Tanager* (Grinnell College), May 1931.

—*POEMS II, Romanticism, Lanterns at Dusk, Vain Longings*, originally published in *The Tanager* (Grinnell College), September 1931.

—*Rendezvous*, originally published in *The Tanager* (Grinnell College), November 1931.

Hunter, Grace.

—*Pheasants*, originally published in *American Mercury Magazine*, Vol. 64, February 1947 and reprinted by permission of Mrs. John Hunter.
—*June Nights*, originally published in *American Mercury Magazine*, Vol. 65, July 1947 and reprinted by permission of Mrs. John Hunter.
—*Release*, originally published in *American Mercury Magazine*, Vol. 65, October 1947 and reprinted by permission of Mrs. John Hunter.
—*Southern Pacific: Golden Trumpet*, originally published in *American Mercury Magazine*, Vol. 69, December 1949 and reprinted by permission of Mrs. John Hunter.

Boyd, Evelyn Mae.

—*Lines*, originally published in *Junto* (Grinnell College), 1924.
—*St. Columb's Eve*, originally published in *Junto* (Grinnell College), 1924.
—*Sea Grief*, originally published in *Junto* (Grinnell College), 1924.
—*Maple Leaves, Arashiyama, Midera*, originally published in *The Tanager* (Grinnell College), November 1926.

Kemmerer, John C.

—*Spring in Winter*, from *Morning and Other Selected Poems by John Kemmerer*, 1971. Copyright © held by Grinnell College.
—*The Wild Plum Tree*, from *Morning and Other Selected Poems by John Kemmerer*, 1971. Copyright © held by Grinnell College
—*Echo*, from *Morning and Other Selected Poems by John Kemmerer*, 1971. Copyright © held by Grinnell College.
—*Wild Prairie Then*, from *Morning and Other Selected Poems by John Kemmerer*, 1971. Copyright © held by Grinnell College
—*Blackberries*, from *Morning and Other Selected Poems by John Kemmerer*, 1971. Copyright © held by Grinnell College.
—*Four Epigrams, Icarus, Novice Reproved, Where the Snow Are, Night Weather*, from *Epigrams: Book One, Book Two, Book Three by John Kemmerer*, 1969. Copyright © held by Grinnell College.

Kauffman, Roma.

—*Garden Paths*, originally published in *The Tanager* (Grinnell College), December 1925.
—*Poems—Two Farewells, Quench the Torch, Symphony in Two Movements (dated respectively December and February)*, originally published in *The Tanager* (Grinnell College), September 1932.

Reid, Augusta Towner.

—*Child on a Hill*, from *Poems and Verses by Augusta Towner Reid*, 1997. Copyright © 1997 by Augusta Towner Reid.

—*A Winter Burial*, from *Westward* by Amy Clampitt. Copyright © 1990 by
Amy Clampitt. Reprinted by permission of Alfred A. Knopf, a division of
Random House Inc.

—*Paumanok*, from *A Silence Opens* by Amy Clampitt. Copyright © 1993 by
Amy Clampitt. Reprinted by permission of Alfred A. Knopf, a division of
Random House Inc.

Pryor, Mary A.

—*Georgia O'Keeffe at Eighty-Four* from *On Occasion, Selected Poems, 1968–92*
by Mary Pryor. Copyright © by Mary Pryor.

—*Monarchs (With apology to Magic Realists and Environmentalists)* from
Moorhead: Not the Film by Mary Pryor, 1996. Copyright © by Mary Pryor.

—*Migration* from *Under Contract* by Mary Pryor, 1995. Copyright © by Mary
Pryor.

—*Ballade for Emily Dickinson*, from *Turnips and Watches* by Mary Pryor, 1998.
Copyright © 1998 by Mary Pryor.

—*If Rain*, from *Turnips and Watches* by Mary Pryor, 1998. Copyright © 1998
by Mary Pryor.

—*Refusal to Buy a Waterbed*, originally published in *Red Weather*, Spring 1994.
Copyright © by Mary Pryor.

Burkett, Mary D. Parsons.

—*A Promise Broken*, originally published in *The Tanager* (1946), Grinnell
College. Copyright © by Mary D. Burkett.

—*Unrequited* from *From Bud to Bloom* by Mary D. Burkett, 1959. Copyright
© by Mary D. Burkett.

—*Post War Plan*, originally published in *The Tanager* (1946 centennial issue),
Grinnell College. Copyright © by Mary D. Burkett.

—*Moon Lib* from *Going to Seed* by Mary D. Burkett, 1996. Copyright © by
Mary D. Burkett.

—*On Snowshoes* from *Going to Seed* by Mary D. Burkett, 1996. Copyright © by
Mary D. Burkett.

—*August Morning* from *Going to Seed* by Mary D. Burkett, 1996. Copyright ©
by Mary D. Burkett.

Harnack, Curtis.

—*The Nearness*, originally published in *The Nation*, Dec. 21, 1985. Copyright
© 1985 by Curtis Harnack.

—*Wearing a Noise Protector in Manhattan*, originally published in *Ontario
Review*, No. 29. Raymond Smith, ed., Princeton, N.J.: Fall–winter, 1988–
1989. Copyright © 1988 by Curtis Harnack.

—*Epithalamium*, originally published in *Chelsea*, 1990. Copyright © 1990 by
Curtis Harnack.

—*Union Square Market*, originally published in *The Nation*, April 20, 1992.
Copyright © 1992 by Curtis Harnack.

—*Early Camera-Work*, originally published in *The Sewanee Review*, 1994.
Copyright © 1994 by Curtis Harnack.

—*Ballet Students in Street-Clothes*, unpublished. Copyright © 2000 by Curtis
Harnack.

420   Schorr, Mark.

—*Graffiti*, from *Post Cards from Gettysburg* by Mark Schorr, self-published, 1999. Copyright © 1999 by Mark Schorr.

—*Beautiful City*, from *Post Cards from Gettysburg* by Mark Schorr, self-published, 1999. Copyright © by Mark Schorr.

—*Babi Yar After 10 Years, for Everett Gendler*, from *Post Cards from Gettysburg* by Mark Schorr, self-published, 1999. Copyright © by Mark Schorr.

—*Kansas Vortex, after Ginsberg's* Wichita Vortex *and in memory of my Grandfather*, Max Schorr, 1858–1918, from Post Cards from Gettysburg by Mark Schorr, self-published, 1999. Copyright © 1999 by Mark Schorr.

—*At the University of Fort Hare, South Africa for Christopher Shaw*, from *Post Cards from Africa* by Mark Schorr, self-published, 1997. Copyright © 1997 by Mark Schorr.

—*To the End of Time*, unpublished. Copyright © 2000 by Mark Schorr.

Heidbreder, Robert.

—*Don't Eat Spiders*, from *Don't Eat Spiders* by Robert Heidbreder. Stoddart Publishing Co. Ltd., Toronto, Canada, 1985 and used by permission of Stoddart. Copyright © 1985 by Robert Heidbreder.

—*Copycat*, from *Don't Eat Spiders* by Robert Heidbreder. Stoddart Publishing Co. Ltd., Toronto, Canada, 1985 and used by permission of Stoddart. Copyright © 1985 by Robert Heidbreder.

—*Today and Yesterday*, from *Don't Eat Spiders* by Robert Heidbreder. Stoddart Publishing Co. Ltd., Toronto, Canada, 1985 and used by permission of Stoddart. Copyright © 1985 by Robert Heidbreder.

—*Peppermint Moose* from *Eenie Meenie Manitoba* by Robert Heidbreder and illustrated by Scot Ritchie, used by permission of Kids Can Press Ltd., Toronto. Text copyright © 1996 by Robert Heidbreder.

—*The Fastest Runner*, from *Python Play and Other Recipes for Fun* by Robert Heidbreder, Stoddart Publishing Co. Ltd., Toronto, Canada, 1999 and used by permission of Stoddart. Copyright © 1999 by Robert Heidbreder.

—*Python Play*, from *Python Play and Other Recipes for Fun* by Robert Heidbreder, Stoddart Publishing Co. Ltd., Toronto, Canada, 1999 and used by permission of Stoddart. Copyright © 1999 by Robert Heidbreder.

Malcolm, River.

—*The Two Goddesses, Persephone, Demeter*, from *No Goddess Dances to a Mortal Tune* by River Malcolm, self-published, 1991. Copyright © 1991 by River Malcolm.

—*The Woman Who Walked on Water*, from *The Woman Who* by River Malcolm, self-published, 1991. Copyright © 1991 by River Malcolm.

—*Looking for My First Kitten*, originally published in *South Coast Poetry*, 1994. Copyright © 1994 by River Malcolm.

Hirsch, Edward.

—*In Spite of Everything, the Stars*, from *Wild Gratitude* by Edward Hirsch. Copyright © 1985 by Edward Hirsch. Reprinted by permission of Alfred A. Knopf, a division of Random House Inc.

—*Days of 1968*, from *On Love* by Edward Hirsch. Copyright © 1998 by Edward Hirsch. Reprinted by permission of Alfred A. Knopf, a division of Random House Inc.

—*Colette*, from *On Love* by Edward Hirsch. Copyright © 1998 by Edward Hirsch. Reprinted by permission of Alfred A. Knopf, a division of Random House Inc.

—*Iowa Flora (In Memory of Amy Clampitt)*, from *On Love* by Edward Hirsch. Copyright © 1998 by Edward Hirsch. Reprinted by permission of Alfred A. Knopf, a division of Random House Inc.

—*Ocean of Grass*, from *On Love* by Edward Hirsch. Copyright © 1998 by Edward Hirsch. Reprinted by permission of Alfred A. Knopf, a division of Random House Inc.

—*After the Last Practice*, copyright © by Edward Hirsch. Originally appeared in *The Kenyon Review* (Winter 1990).

McClaurin, Irma.

—*The Power of Names*, from *Pearl's Song* by Irma McClaurin, Lotus Press, 1988, 2000. Copyright © 1988 by Irma McClaurin.

—*To a Gone Era (My College Days—Class of '73)*, from *Pearl's Song* by Irma McClaurin, Lotus Press, 1988, 2000. Copyright © 1988 by Irma McClaurin.

—*Return to Punta Gorda*, originally published in *The Caribbean Writer*, 1999. Copyright © 1999 by Irma McClaurin.

—*A Mother's Day Blessing*, from *Women of Belize* by Irma McClaurin. Rutgers University Press, 1996. Copyright © 1996 by Irma McClaurin.

—*Childhood Memories*, from *Pearl's Song* by Irma McClaurin, Lotus Press, 1988. Copyright © 1988 by Irma McClaurin.

—*Adieu Poem (In Memory of Duane Casey Taylor '73)*, unpublished. Copyright © 2000 by Irma McClaurin.

Balk, Christianne.

—*Elegy*, from *Bindweed* by Christianne Balk. MacMillan Publishing Co., 1986. Copyright © 1986 by Christianne Balk.

—*Leaving Sand County: April 21, 1948 (Aldo Leopold died on this day while fighting a grass fire.)* from *Bindweed* by Christianne Balk. MacMillan Publishing Co., 1986. Copyright © 1986 by Christianne Balk.

—*Old Minto*, from *Desiring Flight* by Christianne Balk. Purdue University Press, 1995. Copyright © 1995 by Christianne Balk.

—*Dear Hippopotamus*, from *Desiring Flight* by Christianne Balk. Purdue University Press, 1995. Copyright © 1995 by Christianne Balk.

—*Tonga Ridge*, from *Desiring Flight* by Christianne Balk. Purdue University Press, 1995. Copyright © 1995 by Christianne Balk.

—*The Wild Dog's Steps*, from *Desiring Flight* by Christianne Balk. Purdue University Press, 1995. Copyright © 1995 by Christianne Balk.

Clompus, Brad.

—*Camac Bathhouse*, originally published in *Amelia*, Spring 1999. Copyright © 1999 by Brad Clompus.

—*The Far Signals*, originally published in *West Branch*, Bucknell University, 1997. Copyright © 1997 by Brad Clompus.

—*Prohibition*, originally published in *South Dakota Review*, 1998, by University Exchange. Copyright © 1998 by Matt Brennan.

—*Shiftwork in February, at Terre Haute Coke and Carbon*, from *The Music of Exile: Poems by Matthew Brennan*. Wyndham Hall Press, 1994. Copyright © 1994 by Matthew Brennan.

—*Preheating*, from *The Music of Exile: Poems by Matthew Brennan*. Wyndham Hall Press, 1994. Copyright © 1994 by Matthew Brennan.

—*The Three-Bagger*, from *The Music of Exile: Poems by Matthew Brennan*. Wyndham Hall Press, 1994. Copyright © 1994 by Matthew Brennan.

Maire, Mark.

—*Hawks' Wings*, originally published in *Arizona Quarterly*, Tucson, Ariz.: The University of Arizona, 1985. Copyright © 1985 by *Arizona Quarterly* and reprinted with permission.

—*March*, originally published in *Farmer's Market*, Elgin, Ill.: Midwest Farmer's Market Inc., 1998. Copyright © by Mark Maire.

—*Haunted*, originally published in the *Wolf Head Quarterly*, Kansas City, Mo.: 1994. Copyright © by Mark Maire.

—*First Apartment: Dubuque, Iowa for Dennis*, unpublished. Copyright © 2000 by Mark Maire.

—*Solstice*, unpublished. Copyright © 2000 by Mark Maire.

—*Clearing and Colder*, unpublished. Copyright © 2000 by Mark Maire.

Kern, Stephen.

—*Iowa Lurking*, originally published in *MUSE*, 1993. Copyright © by Stephen Kern.

—*Dreams From the Hallway*, originally published in *MUSE*, 1993. Copyright © by Stephen Kern.

—*This Has No Name*, originally published in *The Poetry Connection*. Chicago, Ill.: Chicago Department of Cultural Affairs, 1991. Copyright © by Stephen Kern.

—*Divide, for Joe, whatever he's up to*, unpublished. Copyright © 2000 by Stephen Kern.

—*Leaf Lust*, unpublished. Copyright © 2000 by Stephen Kern.

—*"It is unlawful to duplicate this key."* unpublished. Copyright © 2000 by Stephen Kern.

Silano, Martha.

—*A Trip Through the Yellow Pages: Ba, Be, and so Forth*, to be published by Nightshade Press in *What the Truth Tastes Like* by Martha Silano. Copyright © 2000 by Martha Silano.

—*For a Friend Who Sends Me a Flyer on the Art of Ear Candling and News Her Book Has Arrived*, to be published by Nightshade Press in *What the Truth Tastes Like* by Martha Silano. Copyright © 2000 by Martha Silano.

—*What I Meant to Say Before I Said "So Long," for Dante Alfredo Silano*, to be published by Nightshade Press in *What the Truth Tastes Like* by Martha Silano. Copyright © 2000 by Martha Silano.

Vilen, Anne.

Sink, Susan.

Ford, Kendra.